Brothers of Evil

BROTHERS OF EVIL

John E. Lewis

AVALON BOOKS
THOMAS BOUREGY AND COMPANY, INC.
NEW YORK

PRINTED IN THE UNITED STATES OF AMERICA
BY HADDON CRAFTSMEN, SCRANTON, PENNSYLVANIA

Brothers of Evil

I

The weather-beaten sign above the doors proclaimed that the gray board building was the First National Bank of Cheyenne, Wyoming. Inside the building, wearing their gray dusters, two men stood with drawn six-guns, holding the bank employees and the two customers at bay.

One of the hold-up men tossed a burlap sack across the counter to the bank clerk.

"Here," he said, "fill this up with all

1

your bank notes and hurry it up. If you give me any trouble, I'll gun you down!"

"Yessir. Yessir. Whatever you say," the bank clerk stammered nervously.

Frantically he picked up wrapped bundles of bank notes and stuffed them into the bag. He was looking down the barrel of a very large revolver. The man holding the revolver meant business. The bank clerk intended to do what the man said.

Quickly the bag was filled and the hold-up man stepped forward and grabbed it. He began backing toward the entrance where his companion waited.

One of the customers, an older man with iron-gray hair, saw what he figured was his money going out the door. He had worked many years for what he had saved and he didn't intend to let it slip away so easily.

As the robber neared the door, the older customer waited. When the hold-up man's attention was focused on someone else, the old-timer grabbed for the Colt .44 revolver that was strapped to his hip.

As quick as the old man was, the bank robber in the gray duster was quicker. He saw the movement out of the corner of his eye and spun to his left. As the old man's gun cleared leather, the gunman squeezed the trigger.

The big iron in his hand roared, and the lead slug tore into the older man's chest. A look of pain, horror, and disbelief crossed the victim's face. His six-gun slipped from his hand, clattering to the floor. He choked and gasped and crumpled onto the floor himself.

By now both of the robbers had rushed out to the street.

At the edge of the board sidewalk, a third man in a light-colored duster waited. He was using both hands to hold the reins of three horses. Seeing his partners, he shifted all the reins to his left hand and quickly drew his six-gun with his right.

There was a strong resemblance among the three men. Even the most casual observer could tell that they were related, probably brothers.

Since it was ten in the morning, there were a number of people on the street, some getting supplies for their homes and farms and ranches, some on other errands. But at the moment they were all staring at the robbers, the Gideon brothers.

Known for their greed and brutality, not their finesse or cool heads, the Gideons tended to shoot at the slightest excuse—and often when there was no excuse at all.

It made the Gideons nervous to be stared at by strangers. Suddenly they all opened fire, scattering the crowd. But not everyone escaped safely.

One wounded man was lying on the sidewalk. A woman crouched by his side and screamed.

The three hold-up men swung into their saddles. At that instant one of the townsmen who had taken cover behind a barrel drew his six-gun and began to fire at them.

They turned and fired back, grazing his arm. Then one of the Gideons shot the woman crouching beside the man who'd fallen on the sidewalk. She moaned softly and fell across his body.

The three gunmen fired another volley of shots at the local people, both seen and unseen. Then, in the smell of dust and gunpowder, they galloped down the street and headed south out of Cheyenne.

II

The orange sun was just beginning to set behind the brown-and-green western hills, and dusk was starting to gather over the small Colorado town of Helaman as a lone horseman came riding down the dusty gray main street.

The man had ridden in from the north end of town. The dust that coated both him and his black horse indicated they had been riding for a long distance.

7

In front of the saloon, the rider swung out of the saddle and tethered the horse to the hitching rail. The man was tall and thin, with black hair and a black mustache. But his lean build did not hide his underlying strength.

Entering the saloon, he automatically pulled his Colt .44 up and down in his holster just to make sure it could be drawn easily if need be.

The saloon was fairly well lighted by lanterns fastened to the walls every six feet around the room. It was only six o'clock in the evening and there weren't many people at the saloon yet. One group of men sat at a table playing faro and two men stood at the long bar that stretched across one end of the room. The bartender was the only other person there.

The tall, dust-covered rider walked across the room, his boots echoing hollowly on the floor. But no one even bothered to look up.

"Whiskey," he said when he reached the bar. His voice was husky from all the dust he had ridden through that day.

As the bartender brought the drink to

the newcomer, the man reached over and took a hard-boiled egg from the free-lunch tray on the corner of the bar. He cracked it and began peeling it.

"Been riding long?" the bartender asked conversationally.

The dark, gaunt man put a gold-dollar piece on the bar to pay for his whiskey.

"Been riding all day," he said, his voice deep and quiet. He took a drink of the fiery amber liquid, letting it trickle along his throat and wash down the dust of the road. Then he went on. "I came in from the north."

The bartender nodded. "Come from Denver?" he asked.

"Came from that direction," the stranger said laconically.

The bartender moved down the bar, wiping the wooden top with his towel as he went. There was an occasional bit of conversation from the faro table. Other than that, the room was quiet.

The tall stranger finished peeling the hard-boiled egg and began eating it, washing it down with sips from the whiskey glass.

Suddenly, the double swinging doors opened again. A young man, apparently in his early twenties, came through the doors and walked to the bar, swaggering as he did so. He ordered whiskey in a demanding voice and tossed it down quickly when it was served to him. Then he looked around the room with an arrogant gaze, his eyes finally settling on the gaunt man standing at the bar.

The younger man stared at the first man for several moments. Then, in a loud voice, he said:

"Does your name happen to be Dan Drage?"

The tall man stared back at the younger one, his face showing no expression. He did not answer, and the second man took that as a deliberate affront. His face turned an angry red.

"I'm talking to you, mister," he yelled. "Is your name Dan Drage? I want an answer."

The tall man's eyes narrowed and he shifted his weight slightly, so that his right hand was close to the Colt .44 resting in its low-slung holster.

"Yes," he finally said in his deep voice. "They call me Dan Drage."

The young man sneered.

"I hear that you're supposed to be the fastest gun around," he said, bravado in his voice.

The tall, gaunt man did not answer this obvious challenge. He had no desire to fight the younger man.

The saloon had by now become silent as a tomb. The faro game stopped and everyone in the room was staring at the two men at the bar.

The younger man clearly felt the need to press what he supposed was his advantage. He moved his feet slightly apart and flexed his fingers over the gun butt at his side.

"Well, I don't think that you're so fast," he said in a loud voice, well aware that the other men in the saloon were watching him. "I think I can outdraw you," he continued.

"Don't try it, son," the dark, gaunt man replied, raising his deep voice so he could be sure the other man heard him clearly.

However, the younger man obviously

took this to indicate that Drage was afraid and he, himself, gained some measure of confidence from what he thought was the thin man's cowardice.

"What's the matter?" he taunted, playing to the audience around him. "Are you afraid of me?"

There was no answer from Dan Drage.

"I think I can take you easily, Drage," the man persisted, and it was obvious that anger and frustration were building up in him because of the lack of response from the older man. "Draw, blast you, draw!"

Dan Drage forced himself to remain calm.

"Son," he warned, "don't try it."

But by now the young man had passed the point of reason. His pride was at stake. The other men in the room were watching him. If he backed off now, he would be considered a coward and would lose face.

No, he could not back off now even if he had wanted to. He stepped away from the bar and suddenly his right hand grabbed for the handle of his gun.

His draw was fast, but Dan Drage's

right hand was faster. In one fluid motion, Drage pulled the Colt .44 revolver from its holster, aimed it, thumbed the hammer back, and squeezed the trigger. All without seeming haste, but all very, very rapidly.

The lead slug from Drage's .44 ripped into the young man's chest. He stood quite still for just a few seconds, a shocked look of disbelief slowly coming over his face, and then his knees buckled and his body slowly crumpled to the floor.

There was quiet in the room after the loud echoing of the gun roar. No one spoke; no one moved. Dan Drage looked sadly at the fallen man for a moment, contemplating the waste of such a young life. Then Drage slipped the still-smoking revolver back into its leather holster and, without any comment, turned back to the bar.

The bartender quickly came up to Drage and, whiskey bottle in hand, poured the tall dark man another shot. Drage thanked him and took another hard-boiled egg from the free-lunch tray.

He looked at the bartender for a moment before he spoke, and his voice was thoughtful and soft.

"This is always the way it is," he sighed sadly. "There's always some young coyote around who has to prove he's a big man to himself and to the other people in the town."

The bartender was still looking at Drage in amazement. The awe was evident in his voice as he spoke.

"Mr. Drage, you were fast. Now I've heard your name and I've heard of your reputation, but I've never really believed you were so fast."

Drage quietly peeled the shell from the egg and took a bite of it. The bartender obviously wanted to talk and bask in the reflected glory of this renowned gunslinger.

"He was nothing but a troublemaker in the town of Helaman, Mr. Drage," the bartender gushed on. "His name is Bert Cooper and he was always bragging around about how fast he was. Trying to get everybody around here to draw against him, trying to impress people."

"And so he finally got to prove his speed with a gun," Drage said sadly, glancing down at the young man's body.

"But he sure couldn't beat you, Mr. Drage," the bartender chuckled. "Nobody could ever beat you to the draw."

"They haven't yet," Drage corrected him. "Someday, someone will come along who can draw his gun faster than I can. Then I'll be gone and he'll be the one who's tested by the young fire-eaters from then on."

Dan Drage had no illusion about how fleeting glory could be. He knew he would not be the fastest draw forever. As he got older, his speed would inevitably slow down and someone younger would finally beat him to the draw. Then that person would be constantly challenged by people like young Bert Cooper.

Drage was quiet as he thought about that, and the bartender had nothing more to say at the moment, so he walked back up the bar, wiping the worn surface with his bar towel.

III

It wasn't long before the sheriff came through the swinging doors of the saloon. He glanced around the room, then walked directly to the body, which was still lying on the floor. He stood there briefly and looked down. The young man's gun had fallen to the floor beside him. The sheriff bent down and picked up the revolver, then looked up at Dan Drage. Standing once more, he walked over to Drage.

"I hear this was self-defense," the sheriff said to the lanky man.

"Yes, it was," Drage responded in his soft, deep voice.

"It sure was, Sheriff," the bartender said and moved down the bar again so that he could be involved in the conversation. "Bert Cooper just goaded him and goaded him, and then Bert drew first. Mr. Drage sure outdrew him, though." And the bartender chuckled again, as though the entire situation were nothing but a good joke.

The sheriff turned toward the faro table and called out the names of two of the men sitting there. He asked them to carry the body out of the saloon and take it to the undertaker's parlor. They grumbled about the request and allowed as how it wasn't their responsibility. The sheriff merely stood there and stared firmly at them.

Reluctantly they got up from their card game, lifted the dead man by the legs and arms, and lugged him out of the saloon. After that grisly business had been taken care of, the sheriff came over to the bar again.

"I'm Mack Nielsen," he said by way of introducing himself to the other man.

"My name is Dan Drage."

The two men shook hands and the sheriff said:

"Dan Drage. Yes, I thought I knew you. Your name is pretty well-known in this part of the country."

Drage merely nodded in response. What the sheriff had said was not unusual; most people in this part of the country had heard of him if they were at all alert. He did seem to get around.

"I don't mind telling you, Mr. Drage, that I'm not too happy to have you in the town of Helaman," the sheriff said bluntly. "I'd just as soon you moved on."

Drage sipped the whiskey from his glass. Then he lowered the glass, and a slight grin crossed his face.

"Is there a warrant out for my arrest, Sheriff?" he asked.

The sheriff smiled thinly.

"No," he admitted, "there's no warrant

out on you as far as I know, Mr. Drage.
I'm not telling you to get out of town by
sundown. I'm just telling you that I don't
feel any too comfortable having you
around here. The reason is just the sort
of thing that happened here."

"I know. I know," Drage said sadly, his
dark eyes staring at the sheriff. "I don't
like to go around killing folks either. It's
people like Bert Cooper who keep trailing
me." He drank the rest of the whiskey in
the glass and set it back down on the bar.
"I will move on, though, Sheriff Nielsen.
I have no intention of sticking around the
town of Helaman, Colorado."

"Just what is your business here in
Helaman?" the sheriff asked bluntly but
not unkindly.

Drage stared down at the shorter man
for a moment before answering. He was
wondering if he could confide in Mack
Nielsen. He decided he could.

"I'm looking for three men, Sheriff," he
finally answered.

The sheriff waited for further expla-
nation. He did not try to hurry the other

man. He reached over and took a slice of meat from the lunch tray.

Finally, Drage continued.

"The three men I'm seeking robbed a bank up in Cheyenne, Wyoming. Happened about a week ago. When they came out of the bank, they shot up the town a little. Shot some of the people who were just standing there in the street. Two of those bystanders were my brother and his wife."

"So you're not acting as a lawman who is after these hold-up men for the robbing of the bank?" the sheriff asked.

Drage smiled, his lips turning up beneath his black mustache.

"No, Sheriff," he replied. "I've never been accused of being a lawman. Oh, I've been hired by ranchers to go after cattle rustlers and such. But that still don't make me a lawman."

Now it was the sheriff's turn to smile. He decided that he liked this tall, gangly stranger.

"So you're just having a vendetta with these men?" Sheriff Nielsen said.

"I suppose you could call it a vendetta for want of a better term," Dan Drage said.

"Who are they? Do you know just who you're after?" the sheriff asked.

"Yes. I know who I'm tracking," Drage told him. "They're brothers. The Gideon brothers: Walt, Tubby, and Frank."

"Oh, yes," the sheriff said, "now I remember. I just today got a wanted poster on them and it told about the robbery in Cheyenne. Do you know for sure they came this way? That they're in this part of the country?"

"I've been following them. I've been on their trail," Drage answered. "If they're not in the town of Helaman right at this moment, I'm sure they're not very far away."

"I'd rather not have a bloodbath in the streets of my town," the sheriff said softly but sternly.

Drage said:

"I'm going to get those men, Sheriff, or die trying, and I'll take them any way I can. If they want to surrender peacefully, I'll be willing to take them in for a trial.

But I admit I don't expect that. And since I don't expect it, I'm willing to draw down on them. I honestly do hope they don't mess up the streets of Helaman, but that won't be my decision. It'll be theirs."

"Are you staying someplace here in town?" the sheriff asked, changing the subject.

"No, I'm not," Drage answered. "But I'll be nearby. You'll see me again. You can be sure of that."

"No doubt that's true," said the sheriff. "I'll probably see you whether I want to or not."

But Mack Nielsen was smiling when he said it and they'd parted on a friendly note. They were both on the same side of the fence in this matter. True, the sheriff did not approve of the methods that Dan Drage used and he didn't like having Drage, a known gunslinger, in his town— because he was likely to attract trigger-happy brawlers like Bert Cooper. But Drage had never been known to fight on the side of outlaws. Everything Nielsen had heard about the man showed him to be on the side of law and order, gunslinger though he might be. That was something.

Still, a gunslinger plus three robbers and killers had to add up to trouble. And in the small town of Helaman, Colorado, the sheriff was the only law officer; he had no deputies. So, with one thing and another, he felt a little nervous.

But on the other hand, Sheriff Mack Nielsen was not at all disturbed to know that, if the Gideon brothers came into his area, the well-known and very experienced gunslinger, Dan Drage, would be there to back him up. In fact, that knowledge would help the sheriff sleep better that night.

IV

The three men hunkered down around
the small campfire. They were under a
small overhang that had been cut out of
the face of the rock wall many centuries
ago by the wind and the rain. It protected
them somewhat from the elements while
at the same time allowing the smoke from
the campfire to be wafted away by the
passing breezes.

The men ate their beans and beef jerky

25

from flat tin plates, sopping the last bits up with hard biscuits. They washed their meal down with strong hot coffee.

"Do you think we'd better ride on into Helaman and take a look at the bank and the town before we go in and hit it and take the money?" Tubby Gideon asked.

Tubby was short and stocky, and it was easy to see how he got his nickname. When he had been born, some years before, his parents had named him Aaron, but no one who knew him now was aware of that. For he was known only as Tubby.

"Yeah," his brother Walt answered. "I think we have to ride in and look the town over. We want to glance at the bank and we want to take a gander at the local sheriff and see what kind of a threat he's going to be."

"I still think that we should have stopped in Denver," Frank grumbled. "There's always bigger banks in a bigger city. Bigger banks and more money."

If Tubby was the butterball of the trio, Frank was the bean pole, while Walt's build was more or less medium. But all three had the same round, ruddy-cheeked face, the same sandy-colored curly hair.

Walt scoured his tin plate with gravel to clean it off after he had eaten.

"Sure," he said in response to Frank's comment about Denver, "there are bigger banks and more money in bigger cities. There are also lots more lawmen there too."

"Well, I'm not afraid of the marshal of Denver, anyway," Frank said. "I'm not afraid of nobody."

Walt stopped cleaning the tin plate and turned to his brother. He jabbed a finger at Frank for emphasis as he spoke.

"You just listen to me. It don't matter if you're scared. It don't matter if you're fast. If you've got lotsa men pointing their six-guns at you, one of them might make you dead. You don't always have to be the fastest gun or the best shot. Sometimes people are just lucky with a gun, and you don't want to be there when they happen to get lucky."

Frank looked at his brother and just mumbled something to himself. Walt was the recognized leader of the three brothers. He wasn't the oldest and they hadn't ever taken a vote on it. He just sounded like the smartest of the three—which wasn't saying much—and so it had worked out that way. He always somehow took over and led them and told them what to do. And the other two followed and did what he told them.

After the three men had cleaned up their plates, they sat around the small fire with their tin coffee cups in their hands. It had become dark by now and the fire cast its light up against the rock wall and the faces of the men.

"All right," Walt said, asserting his authority, "here's what I want you to do. We'll ride into town first thing in the morning. Frank, you'll go to the bank and just get a couple of bills changed. Get the layout of the bank down and see what's the best way to go in and how we can get away after. Tubby, I want you to go to the sheriff's office."

"The sheriff's office?" Tubby asked incredulously. "Why would I want to go there?"

"Yes, the sheriff's office," Walt repeated. "Tell the sheriff that you just rode

in from the south and ask directions on
how to get to Denver from here. While
you're in his office, take a look around.
Find out if he has any deputies and see if
you can get a feel for how good he is. You
know, how old he is, how strong he is, how
sharp. Find out just what we're up against
as far as the law goes in the town of Helaman."

"Yeah. Yeah. I get you," Tubby said.
"It's just that I don't like being around
lawmen."

"What'll you be doing while we're doing
all this?" Frank asked. It wasn't a challenge. It was just a question, asked out of
curiosity.

"Oh, I'll be checking out the town gen-
erally," Walt told him. "I'll ride around
the streets and find the best way into and
out of the town. I'll be looking at the back
alleys and things like that. When the
three of us get through spending the day
there, we'll have a pretty good idea of how
to take that there bank and how to get
away fast."

Dan Drage sat by his own small campfire less than a mile away from the Gideon brothers. But he didn't know he was that close to them. He just knew they were somewhere nearby.

Dan too had finished his supper. Now he sat quietly by the dying embers of the small fire and just watched the stars and thought—mostly about the Gideon brothers, who outnumbered him three to one and were known to be real fast with their six-guns.

V

Early the next morning, after they had eaten breakfast and cleaned up their campsite, the three Gideon brothers rode into the town of Helaman and split up.

Frank went to the town bank, Tubby headed toward the sheriff's office, and Walt casually rode around the streets of the town. Not that there were that many streets in the town, since Helaman was not a booming metropolis. In fact, it wasn't even a very large town compared to some other Colorado towns. But big or small, Walt wanted to know it as well as he could.

Dan Drage had also ridden into town. He stopped at one of the small cafes to have breakfast. After he finished eating and walked outside, he ran right into a man walking in the opposite direction. He started to apologize. Then the two looked at each other for a moment and recognition flashed across the faces of both.

"Dan Drage!" the other man said.

"Eli Quartz!" Drage responded, and the two shook hands warmly.

"Are you still preaching hellfire and brimstone for a living?" Drage asked the other man.

"Yes," was the response. "I'm riding the circuit a bit, preaching in the towns around about here. Helaman is my home base, though. I have a small church just down the street here."

"Well, I am glad to see that you're still around," Drage told him. "I was afraid that some sinner might have gotten to you a long time ago."

"Listen," Quartz replied, "if associating with you over the years didn't do me in, then no other sinner could get me."

The two men laughed together.

"What are you doing down here in the town of Helaman, Dan?" the minister then asked him.

"Well, I'm not on the same kind of mission that you are, Eli," Drage responded. "I'm here riding after three men. They're known as the Gideon brothers. They robbed a bank up in Cheyenne and, in the shootout that took place, they killed my brother Gabe and his wife Mary."

"Oh, Dan, I'm real sorry about that."

"I know you are, Eli. You are one of the people who care about others," Drage said.

"But you're not a lawman now, are you?" the preacher asked. "Why are you pursuing them?"

Drage looked off at the distant hills and there was a deep sadness in his eyes. He hesitated for a few minutes before answering.

"Eli," he finally said with solemnity in his voice, "I'm going to get these men because they killed my brother and his wife. It doesn't have anything to do with law work. That shouldn't be too hard to figure out."

Quartz was also solemn as he responded. He recognized the pain that his friend had. But his own moral code was something that he could not ignore and he felt compelled to make a point.

"You know what it says in the Good Book, Dan," Quartz said. "It says, 'Vengeance is Mine. I will repay.'"

Drage stroked his chin and looked at Eli Quartz. He did not want to argue with his friend and he especially did not want to argue in the area of religion, since he knew how strongly Quartz felt about that. However, Drage had his own set of values and he felt that he could not ignore his sense of justice.

"Eli," he finally said, "I honestly believe that vengeance is a thing of God. But I also believe that He works through men. I tend to believe that I can be an instrument by which that vengeance can be worked."

The minister smiled wryly and put his hand on the arm of his tall, lean friend.

"I would be one of the last people to question your motives, Dan," he said. "But are you sure you aren't just letting your anger carry you away?"

"I have to do what I have to do, Parson," Drage said. "And I really don't feel any need to apologize to anyone for seeking revenge for the murder of my brother and his wife. I was just saying that about being a tool of vengeance for your benefit, to make you feel better about things. I really feel quite sure about what I'm doing."

The minister laughed at that. He had forgotten the stubbornness that Drage had shown over the years. When Drage got an idea about something, it was almost impossible to change his mind.

"Okay, okay," Eli said somewhat ruefully. "So much for my lecture and sermonizing."

"Come on," Drage said, smiling, "it's fine for you to have gotten religion, Eli,

but I don't think you should forget your
old friends or your background completely. You ought to try to keep things
in perspective. You and I did an awful lot
of riding and shooting together. Neither
one of us felt the need to justify our actions back then."

"Well, that's true," the minister said
with a smile. "But I am hoping that I have
progressed a little and found a better way
since those days."

"I hope for your sake you've found what
you consider a better way," Drage said.
"But I don't think you ought to be judging
my actions because of the way you've cho-
sen."

The minister clapped Drage on the
shoulder and his smile had turned to an
open boyish grin.

"That's another thing the Bible teaches,
Dan. We shouldn't judge one another. I
would never deliberately put myself in
the position of judging you, and you know
it."

"Sure. I know that, Eli," Drage said.
"Well, why don't you come into the saloon
with me and I'll buy you a beer. That is,

if you still drink, with all of the religion you've got."

Eli Quartz laughed loudly at that.

"Sure. I'll still drink a beer with you."

VI

Dan Drage and Eli Quartz walked into the nearby saloon together. They ordered beers and the bartender recognized the tall, gaunt gunslinger from the night before and started to go on about the shoot-out until Drage stopped him. Drage didn't feel that he needed any more talk on the subject. He was forced, though, to explain to his friend what had happened the night before.

"That's one of the problems, isn't it, Dan?" Quartz said. "When you deal in guns and shooting, this thing always follows you."

"That's true, Eli," Drage admitted. "I haven't been able to get away from it, and I don't know if I ever will."

At the same time that Drage and Quartz were reminiscing over a couple of cool beers at the saloon, Walt Gideon was riding up one of the side streets of the town. He had been riding up and down the streets for some time to get a look at things. Now he swung down from his horse to have a better, closer look around the town.

He looped the horse's reins over the hitching rail and began to walk along the streets. He looked to the right and to the left with a studied casual glance, checking the streets, alleys, and buildings. Helaman looked just about the same as any other small western town and Walt Gideon made note of the entrances, exits, and taller buildings around. He hoped he could remember it all when the time came.

Moving along Main Street, Walt Gid-

eon appeared to be casual and relaxed.
Suddenly, however, he stiffened and his
right hand automatically dropped to the
wooden gun butt. He had seen Sheriff
Mack Nielsen walking down Main Street
toward him.

Gideon did not know the sheriff personally. He had never seen the man before in his life, but the silver badge that
was pinned to the sheriff's vest caught the
sunlight and glinted brightly. The star of
the lawman was hard to miss, especially
by someone like Walt Gideon who had
spent a lifetime being on the lookout for
lawmen.

Without thinking—just knowing in his
gut that all lawmen were his enemies—
Walt pulled his gun quickly from its holster.

At that point, the sunlight glinted off
the barrel of Walt's gun and Sheriff Nielsen's attention was drawn to it. His own
right hand flashed like lightning to the
big iron on his hip, but, unfortunately, it
was too late.

Walt Gideon had already taken aim and
the lead slug spun toward its target.

Sheriff Mack Nielsen was fairly fast with a gun, but his revolver was only half out of its holster when the bullet from Gideon's gun struck him in the chest. Intense pain wracking his body, the sheriff slowly crumpled to the ground. Then he was motionless.

Women bystanders screamed and one of the men on the sidewalk cursed, but no one had the presence of mind to act. Very quickly Walt Gideon turned on his heel and ran back to the side street where his horse was tethered.

He scrambled into the saddle, grabbed up the reins, and spurred his mount into motion. He still had the six-gun in his hand and, as he galloped away, he fired a few more shots at random, just to keep the bystanders at bay and to keep anyone from firing at him. His shots had the desired effect on the populace. No one moved and Walt Gideon made his getaway without being challenged.

VII

Seconds later, Dan Drage and Eli Quartz burst through the saloon doors and ran down the street toward the crumpled figure of Sheriff Mack Nielsen.

A woman who had been loading supplies in a wagon in front of the general store ran toward the sheriff and reached him just as the two men did. Dan Drage bent down and examined Nielsen. He felt for the pulse in the neck, but he could detect no sign of the heart beating. There was no pulse.

Drage thought wryly about his recent conversation with the sheriff. How ironic it was that it was the sheriff's own body that was now on the street. Dan looked up at Quartz and at the woman standing there.

"He's dead," Drage said somberly.

The preacher swore.

"Parson!" the woman said, shock showing in her voice that the minister had exhibited such a human trait.

"I'm sorry," Quartz told her penitently, "but he was such a good man. This is a terrible waste."

Then the minister realized that the woman and Drage did not know each other. As ludicrous as it was, over the body of the dead sheriff, Quartz introduced them.

"Miss Marie Sandoval, I would like to present Dan Drage. Marie is one of the cattle ranchers in this area, Dan." Then to the woman, Eli said, "Dan Drage is one of my oldest friends. I have known him for a long time."

Drage doffed his hat as they were introduced.

"I am pleased to meet you, ma'am," he said. "I do wish that the circumstances of our meeting could have been more pleasant."

"Yes," she said, looking down at the body of Sheriff Mack Nielsen and shuddering involuntarily. "There could have been more pleasant circumstances."

"Miss Sandoval," Drage said, "tell me what happened here. What did you see?"

"A man—a man came down the street from there." And she pointed at the side street. "And he just pulled a gun and shot the sheriff. It seemed like it was for no reason at all." She was trembling as she talked. "The sheriff didn't have a chance," she went on. "He didn't even see the man until just before he was shot."

"Did you get a chance to see the man?" Drage asked in his low, quiet tone.

She looked into his face and the tears were evident in her eyes as she spoke.

"Yes. He was sort of average in size—shorter than you. And he had curly sandy-colored hair."

Drage looked quickly at Eli Quartz.

"The description sounds like it could be Walt Gideon!" he said.

"Probably is," the minister replied.

"Do you know this man?" Marie Sandoval asked Drage.

"If it's who I think it is, then I do," he responded. "He's a killer, and he's not alone. He has two brothers traveling with him. I've followed them from Wyoming. They robbed a bank and killed some people there."

"Are you a lawman?" she asked.

He smiled a thin smile. That certainly seemed to be a popular question for people to be asking him these days.

"No," he answered shortly. "I am not a lawman."

"He's on a vengeance trail, Marie," Quartz said. "These men killed his brother and his brother's wife when they robbed the bank up in Cheyenne."

"Then I don't blame you for being after them," the dark-haired woman said to Drage. She looked down again at the body of the sheriff. "I hope you get those men

and I hope you make them pay for all of
the evil they've done."

"I certainly intend to do just that," the
tall, wiry man replied laconically.

At that moment the town undertaker
arrived with his wagon. Eli Quartz as-
sisted him and they got the body of the
sheriff onto the wagon.

While that grisly task was being taken
care of, Drage escorted Marie Sandoval
back to her own wagon. She had already
loaded her supplies onto the vehicle so
Drage helped her cover the boxes with a
canvas to keep the dust out. He lashed a
rope across and tied it to the wagon bed.
Then he helped her up to the seat and
handed her the reins.

"Are you going to be in Helaman long,
Mr. Drage?" she asked.

"You can be sure that I'll be here long
enough to get the job done," he told her.
Then he added with a smile, "I hope that
I see you again, Miss Sandoval."

"I'll be looking forward to that," she answered. "Well, I have a visit or two to
make here in town. By the way, my spread

is down the main road to the south about
five miles. Then you take the road to the
west."

"Since I'll be looking for those killers
around the entire area, I may get down
that way," Drage said.

"Stop in," she responded. "We'll have a
cup of coffee together."

He touched the brim of his hat and she
waved to him, then slapped the reins along
the horses' backs, starting them in motion. He watched her for a few minutes
as she drove away.

Then he turned to Eli Quartz, who was
waiting for him.

"Just why would Walt Gideon gun down
the sheriff like that?" the minister mused.
"From what Marie said, the sheriff hadn't
even seen him. He couldn't have faced him
down."

Drage shrugged his shoulders.

"Who knows?" he said. "Maybe he was
afraid that the sheriff would spot him and
be able to identify him. Maybe he pan-
icked when he saw the star on the sheriff's chest. For that matter, maybe he's
just a mad-dog killer who shoots at all

lawmen every time he gets the slightest chance."

"Do you believe that about him?" Quartz asked.

"I don't know," Drage said, shaking his head. "I really don't know. Maybe it's just that he was afraid of being identified. By the way," he went on, "just who is second in command in the law department in this town? Does the sheriff have a deputy?"

"No," the minister said. "The town council has to meet and select another sheriff now. Until they do that, the United States marshal for Colorado has jurisdiction in the town."

"And just where is he located, in case we wanted to get in touch with him in a hurry?" Drage asked.

"The office is located in Denver, but they have a sub-office in Colorado Springs," Quartz said. "Neither of which is very close in case of emergency. They may send someone down here when they find out that the sheriff has been killed, but I wouldn't count on any immediate help."

Dan Drage stroked his angular chin.

"Hmmm," he mused, "if someone were

going to hit the bank and they knew what the situation was in the town of Helaman, this would be a very good time to strike, wouldn't it?"

Eli Quartz looked at him thoughtfully and pondered the point himself.

"It would," the minister said. "It certainly would."

VIII

After he had gunned down the sheriff
and gotten to his horse, Walt Gideon rode
as hard as he could out of Helaman, heading to the east and then circling back toward the south. He rode as though
someone was behind him, since he was
sure that a posse would be following him.

However, when he topped a rise a couple of miles out of town, he looked over
his shoulder and could see no one behind

him. Since there was no one close, and since there was no advantage in pushing his horse so hard that it would be injured, Walt allowed it to slow down.

He could see the town in the distance and there did appear to be some activity taking place on the streets. But he still did not see any men on horseback, so he didn't think he was being pursued.

Glancing behind him often, Gideon rode down the trail until he came to the gray rock overhang where he and his brothers had spent the night before. He looked around quickly, but he could see no one. Apparently, his two brothers were not back yet, so Walt dismounted. He led the horse into a stand of scrub oak and tethered it.

After that he made his way back to the overhang and sat behind a rock where he could not be seen by any chance observers. Then he drew his six-gun, swung the cylinder open, extracted the spent casings, and slowly and deliberately reloaded the weapon.

He had just finished slipping the last bullet into the revolver when he heard the sound of horses' hooves on the dry, hard road. Immediately Walt Gideon became alert. He trained the pistol toward the road and was ready for whoever might come.

He sat quietly until he heard the voice of his brother Frank softly calling to him:

"Walt. Hey, Walt. Are you in there?"

"Yeah. Yeah, I'm here," he answered.

The other two men dismounted when they heard his voice. They slipped their six-guns back into their holsters. Then they led their own horses over to the scrub oak where Walt had tethered his. When they finally had the horses taken care of, the other two men joined Walt by the overhang.

Tubby took his hat off and wiped his forehead with his sleeve. Then he sat down on one of the rocks and looked at his brother Walt.

"Boy, you sure set off some ruckus in that town there, killing that sheriff like you did," Tubby said. "There's really some hullabaloo going on down there."

"Yeah, why'd you go and do that for?" Frank asked, obvious pique in his voice.

Frank was the oldest of the three and, even though they all acknowledged Walt as the leader, when it seemed appropriate to challenge Walt's decisions, it was Frank that did the challenging and the talking. "It seems kind of dumb to just go out and gun down a lawman."

"I didn't have no choice. He was coming right down the street at me," Walt said defensively. "There are wanted posters out on us and how'd I know but that the hick sheriff wouldn't recognize me."

He got up and paced up and down. He did not like being questioned by his brothers, or by anybody else for that matter. He was the leader. He had helped them be a successful team in robbing banks all through Wyoming, Colorado, and Utah. He didn't figure that they had any right to talk to him this way.

"Anyway," he finally said, "it's done. I did what I thought was best. The only good sheriff is a dead sheriff, and I made sure that that one is a good sheriff."

Tubby wiped his forehead with his sleeve again. It would have been obvious even to the most casual observer that

Tubby was the most nervous one of the
group. He was the one who was the most
fearful among the brothers.

"Don't you think we'd better haul our-
selves out of here?" Tubby asked. "Maybe
we oughta head south. We could ride into
New Mexico, or maybe even get clear out
of the country into old Mexico. They
couldn't get us there. They'll be getting a
posse out after us, you can bet on that."

And he wiped his forehead with his
sleeve again, as though for emphasis.

Walt quit pacing and squatted down on
the ground. He picked up a stick and began to draw lines in the dust on the
ground, thinking the problem out and
trying to keep himself under control so
that he could convince his brothers what
to do and that they should still follow his
leadership.

"Well, I dunno," he finally said. "Did
either of you hear of any other lawmen in
the town?"

Frank sat down on a rock beside his two
brothers. Tubby was still wiping his brow.

"I went over to the office like you told
me," Tubby said. "But it was locked up.

A note said that the sheriff was out of the office."

"Now that you mention it," Frank said, "I heard somebody in the town say that the sheriff didn't have no deputies. It's kind of a small town, you know."

Walt grinned. They were back with him now and he knew it. It didn't take him long to reassert his leadership when he put his mind to it.

"This thing in this town might be playing right into our hands," Walt said.

"What do you mean?" Tubby asked.

"Well, most of these small towns don't organize a posse unless the sheriff is around to do it. Your average, small general-store operator ain't going to take it upon himself to get a posse up and go out after somebody. If there ain't no sheriff or deputy in the town, there ain't likely to be no posse."

"Hey, you know that's right," Tubby said in amazement, as though he had just received some divine revelation.

Frank chuckled. "That also means that right now there ain't no protection to speak of in the town of Helaman either."

"Right," Walt replied, starting to warm to his subject now that they were with him again. "There's no protection in the town and there's no protection at the bank either. If we're going to hit the bank at Helaman, now will be the time to do it!"

Tubby was still the most insecure of the brothers. He got up and nervously wiped his forehead. He was always the one who was fearful that things just wouldn't go quite right. Now he was again playing the part of the devil's advocate.

"I don't know, Walt," he said, with the obvious hint of a quaver in his voice. "People in that town might be up in arms because their sheriff has been killed. They might be waiting for us."

"Aw, Tubby, the people in town will be scared to death," Walt scoffed. "This is exactly the time when we can show our power. There ain't nobody down in that town that will dare to stand up to us or resist us. They'll all run."

Frank slapped his knee with his new-found enthusiasm. "Yeah, boy, I think you're right," he said.

Being the insecure one, Tubby was usually fearful, but he was also usually very easily swayed by his brothers. He did not like to go against their wishes and he did not like to show any real opposition to the things they said or did. Since both of his brothers seemed so convinced that they were right about this, he quickly fell into line with their thinking, although he did not adopt it as enthusiastically as they had.

"Well, if we're going to hit the bank, I guess this would be about as good a time as any," Tubby said.

Walt slapped him on the back to show that there were no hard feelings and that the three of them were united.

"You bet it would be a good time. Now you're talking!" Walt said. "We're going to be leaving this town of Helaman a lot richer than we were when we came here. Now let's make some plans."

IX

Dan Drage and his preacher friend Eli Quartz were in the small sheriff's office together. Quartz paced up and down. He was obviously very upset that Sheriff Mack Nielsen had been shot.

As the preacher paced up and down, Dan Drage sat quietly behind the old, scarred wooden desk, watching him. Drage was also upset by the killing of the sheriff. He was further upset because he

had not been able to find those Gideons
and bring them to bay before they had
killed again.

But instead of moving about restlessly,
Drage seemed very still, almost frozen.
The only outward sign of his emotional
turmoil was the way his fingers kept
drumming on the desk top as he sat there.

The door to the office opened and Eli
Quartz stopped in mid-pace. The attractive
dark-haired woman, Marie Sandoval,
came into the room. She looked at Drage
sitting behind the desk and quickly
jumped to a conclusion.

"Are you the new sheriff?" she asked
him, and it was obvious that she was hoping he was by the way her face lighted
up.

A slight smile crossed Drage's lips. It
seemed as if everyone was confusing him
with a lawman these days. He swept his
hat off in the presence of the lady.

"No, my dear," he said, "although I
thank you for what's probably meant to
be a compliment. In the past, no one ever
seriously accused me of being a lawman."

"That's too bad," she said. "The town of

Helaman could use a man like you to look after it."

"That's certainly true," the minister said. "Dan's very capable and could do the job."

"Thank you both," Drage told them. "As I said, I'm sure that's intended to be a compliment and I'll accept it as such. But law work just doesn't seem to be cut out for me and I suspect I'll continue to avoid it in the future as I have in the past."

Then he looked directly at Marie Sandoval. "Are you headed out to your ranch now?" he asked her, more to change the subject than anything.

"Yes," she answered. "I'm going out there now. I could see that there was someone here in the office so I came in to find out what was happening."

"Well, we haven't accomplished anything yet," Drage said. "But we will. I'm sure that I'll see you again," he went on. "I'm going to be around here until the job is done."

She studied him as he spoke. He was not an unattractive man, although he looked as if he could use a good meal. He did give the appearance of self-assurance and it was comforting to see that. She flushed slightly when she realized that she was staring at him so directly.

"I'll be looking forward to seeing you again," she told him, and she really meant it.

Marie turned then and went out.

"A nice woman, that Miss Sandoval," Drage said after she had left. "Pleasant and attractive."

"Yes, she is," the minister agreed. "You know," he added, "her idea isn't a bad one."

Drage smiled. "Which idea? That I become the sheriff of Helaman, Colorado?" he asked.

"Yes," Quartz said. "I'm sure that the mayor and the other town leaders would be very happy to have you in that position. In fact, I'd be happy to go to them and talk to them about it if you'd agree to accept."

The tall dark man smiled his enigmatic smile again as he looked at his friend.

"Eli, Eli," he said good-naturedly, "as our Indian friends would say, 'You speak with a forked tongue.' You've accused me of being engaged in a six-gun vendetta against these Gideons. Then at the same time you tell me I should be a lawman."

"You'd be a good lawman," Quartz said, "and you know it. You have a lot of the characteristics of a good sheriff."

Drage slowly unfolded his lanky frame from the chair and stood up behind the desk. He walked to the small window and looked out. The street looked normal and the people were walking by as though nothing out of the ordinary had ever happened. It was interesting, Drage thought, how easy it was for people to slip back into their ruts and forget, or ignore, the unpleasant things that happened around them. Maybe, though, that was how people survived.

"I can't be held down by the ties of the law, Eli," Dan finally said to the minister. "I have to be free to go after people like these Gideon brothers without any restraints on me. Who knows? I may even want to draw first against them if I get the chance. Good lawmen aren't supposed to do things like that. That's why I wouldn't make a good sheriff and why I don't want to be one."

"Where do you think the Gideon brothers are now?" the parson asked. "Do you think they've hightailed it out of the country?"

"No," Drage said. "They're still close around. You can bet your next week's paycheck on that. They're going to hit this town. The sheriff is gone now and they have a prime chance to rob the bank without any resistance. I'm willing to bet that they'll ride in here in the next forty-eight hours, hot and ready to hit the bank."

"And, of course, they don't know that you're here in town," the minister said.

"Right. I'm sure they don't know that I'm around. And they wouldn't care if they did. They've likely heard of me. They know I'm fast on the draw. But so are they, so are they. And there's three of them."

"So what are you going to do, Dan?" Quartz asked him.

"I'm not really sure, Eli," Drage responded. "I do know I have to do something. But the robbers have the advantage. They know how and when they're going to make their move. We

don't. Right now we just have to watch
out and wait."

X

Early the next morning Dan Drage, who'd spent the night at the minister's house, was riding out of town, headed north. He wanted to find the Gideon brothers before they made their expected raid on the town of Helaman and its Wells Fargo Bank. There was no particular reason why Dan Drage rode to the north of the town. He simply didn't know which direction to choose, so he chose that one first. After all, the Gideons might be hiding in the hills there.

After a while, Drage paused in the shade of some pale-green juniper trees. He carefully scanned the valley below him and the hills on either side. He could see the town of Helaman. It was a typical small western community on a typical summer morning.

Drage sat there for a time and then he decided to ride around the surrounding foothills, working his way toward the south end of the valley. He urged his horse into motion when suddenly he saw some movement clear across the valley to the south. Looking hard, Drage could make out three horsemen riding toward the town of Helaman.

Obviously, at that distance he could not see who the men were, yet there was no question in his mind but that they were the three Gideon brothers. Since they were on the south side of the valley and Dan Drage was on the north end, he was in precisely the wrong place at the right time.

Annoyed at himself, Dan Drage swore

loudly and fluently. He kicked his horse in the flanks and slapped the reins across its neck.

Charging down the hillside, Drage really had no illusions about getting down to the town in time to stop the Gideons from robbing the bank. He only hoped that he would make it in time to stop them from getting away afterward—if they didn't kill him first.

His horse stumbled and then recovered, and Drage realized that he had to slow down a little if he didn't want to risk losing the animal. So he eased off slightly on the reins and cut the speed of the horse to a more reasonable rate. But he was still mad at himself for having ridden to the north of the town instead of the south.

Walt, Frank, and Tubby Gideon rode up the main street of the town of Helaman. They tried to look as casual as possible—with Walt flanked by the other two—and not to seem in a hurry. They did not want anyone to take particular notice of them.

As a matter of fact, they did not arouse

any particular interest from the people on the street. Tubby and Frank had not really been noticed by anyone yesterday, and Walt was practically hidden by the other two. Besides, a lot of strangers passed through town without creating a great deal of curiosity.

The three men rode up in front of the bank and dismounted. As they had previously planned, Tubby stood by the hitching rail, trying to look casual as he held the reins of the three horses.

But he really couldn't relax. He glanced up and down the street quickly and often, and his nervousness would have been apparent if anyone had been watching him closely. No one was watching, though.

Walt and Frank walked up the steps and went into the bank. Walt walked up to the window where the clerk was seated, and Frank took his place to the side of the door. There were only four people in the bank: the manager, the bank clerk, and two customers.

Simultaneously, after a signal from Walt, Walt and Frank drew their six-guns.

Walt leveled his revolver across the

counter at the clerk and said:

"This is a holdup. I want you to take all the money in the drawer and put it in two or three of your bank bags. If you don't do what I tell you, I'll kill you."

"Don't anybody try to be a hero!" Frank said loudly, just to let them know that he was by the door and had his own pistol trained on them.

"You two lie down on the floor," Frank said to the two customers, waving his gun barrel at them for emphasis.

The two men quickly complied with his demand.

The manager was a small, nervous, balding man. He fidgeted restlessly while the clerk was filling the bags with money. It would have been obvious to someone watching the manager that he was thinking of making some kind of a move. But Walt Gideon was not watching the manager that closely. He was more intent on what the clerk was doing.

The two men on the floor lay motionless. When the clerk had filled the bank bags with money, he pushed them across the counter.

Walt Gideon took the bags in his left arm and said:

"All right, where's the safe?"

"It's right back—" the clerk began.

But the manager cut him off in mid-sentence.

"No!" he screamed. "You can't have that money! I'm responsible for it. You can't have it!"

And he ran toward the back of the small bank where the safe was located. Before Walt Gideon could get a good aim at him, the manager grabbed the huge iron door of the wall safe—which had carelessly been left open—and slammed it shut. Gideon pushed the bank clerk aside and aimed his gun at the manager.

Just as the manager turned the dial on the safe, Walt Gideon fired, the gun roaring like thunder in the confined space. The bank manager clutched his shoulder and fell to the floor, moaning.

"Nobody try anything else!" Walt Gideon shouted, furious because they'd have to forget the contents of the safe.

The hapless bank clerk dropped unceremoniously to the floor, his arms wrapped over his head, as though he could protect himself that way. The two customers did not move at all from their inglorious positions on the floor.

Walt Gideon backed slowly toward the door, watching the men inside the bank carefully. By now Frank had the front door open. Walt fired one more shot into the ceiling, just as a warning. Then the two backed out the door and headed for the horses.

All three brothers quickly mounted. They fired several shots in the air just to discourage any bystanders from getting too close to them.

XI

As Dan Drage neared the town, he heard gunshots and knew that the bank robbery was already in progress. He urged his horse to move faster.

Drage charged into Helaman noticing the white-faced citizens hiding inside stores and behind barrels and wagons. His horse's hooves skidded on the hard road and beat a tattoo as he turned a street corner and headed toward the bank. He drew his Colt .44 from the holster as he rode.

He could see the three men already in their saddles when he approached the bank. They fired at him quickly as they turned their horses and rode off in three different directions, so that he could not follow all of them.

Drage leveled his weapon and fired back, and Frank Gideon's horse went down. The man leaped from the falling animal and ran between two of the nearby buildings, his six-gun still in his hand.

The other two brothers were far away, so Drage quickly decided to go after Frank. He'd catch up with the others later.

He swung off his horse and merely dropped the reins on the hitching rail at the bank, knowing the animal would not stray.

Just then a distraught bank clerk stepped out of the bank.

"Is anybody hurt?" Drage asked the pasty-face man.

"Mr. Sowards has been shot by those ruffians," the clerk said. "But he's still alive."

"Then hurry and go get the doctor, man," Drage ordered.

The bank clerk left on the run, anxious to be someplace else, happy that someone had given him the authority to leave this place of recent violence.

Drage looked around him, his Colt poised and ready. He wasn't sure which way the one Gideon brother had run after his horse had gone down.

A small boy crept out from behind a nearby watering trough and sensed what Drage wanted to know. He pointed between two nearby buildings.

"He went that way, mister," the boy shouted.

"Thank you," Drage said and moved quickly down the narrow pathway between the two buildings.

His dark eyes scanned the area immediately in front of him and he glanced quickly at the tops of the buildings also. He saw nothing.

Beyond the buildings was an open field. An empty field.

There were a few trees in the field, but they were too small to conceal a grown man. No, Gideon wasn't hidden behind any of them. Drage now glanced along the backs of several other buildings as he stood in the field. He still saw nothing.

Unhappy at the way things were going, Drage started walking behind the row of buildings, ever vigilant, ever alert for the slightest sound or movement.

Further up, he saw that the small back door of the church was slightly ajar. It might mean nothing, but it deserved further checking. He moved up slowly.

Meanwhile, inside the church, Frank Gideon was facing Eli Quartz, and Gideon had his six-shooter trained on the minister.

"You can't get away with this, you know," Quartz said. "You're trapped here in this town."

Frank Gideon laughed, but it was laughter without humor.

"Parson, we *have* gotten away with it," he said in reply. "We got the money from the bank and we're going far away from this hick town. All I need is another horse and I'll be gone."

"My horse is kept down at the stable,"

the minister said. "I don't have one here at the church." He reached out his hand. "Here. Give me your gun. Don't continue your work of evil. Turn yourself in."

Eli Quartz was not a naive man. He knew that he was not going to make Frank Gideon repent in the next few seconds. He was stalling, hoping that Frank might let down his guard and he could wrest the weapon from him.

Gideon lifted the barrel of the revolver slightly and pointed it menacingly at Eli Quartz's face.

"Don't press me, holy man," he snarled. "The only thing I need to do right now is to get a horse and ride out of this town. And I'll do that in spite of you or anybody else. If you get in my way—if you take one step toward me—I'll kill you!"

"But you know that killing people isn't the answer to anything," Quartz answered in what he hoped was a soothing tone.

Then the minister made a fatal mistake. He took that one step toward Frank Gideon.

Gideon was as good as his word. He

acted immediately. His six-gun roared and the bullet struck Eli Quartz full in the chest. The minister gasped with shock and pain. He staggered and slowly slipped to the floor.

Dan Drage had just reached the small back door to the old church building when he heard the roar of the gun. He quickly threw the door all the way open and stepped inside.

Frank Gideon saw movement at the back door and immediately swung his revolver around. He pulled the trigger hard, but in his haste he pulled it too hard, jerking the weapon, and the bullet went wild and struck the doorjamb.

Dan Drage's Colt .44 was already raised. He aimed it carefully and deliberately, and squeezed the trigger slowly. The Colt roared and kicked back against the palm of his hand. Frank Gideon jerked. His knees buckled and he clutched at the spot that was blossoming bright crimson on his chest. Then his body slumped to the floor.

Dan Drage holstered his six-gun and moved quickly to the side of his friend,

Eli Quartz. Drage knelt on the floor and lifted Quartz's head onto his lap.

"Hang on, Eli," Drage told him. "I'll get the doctor here right soon. You're going to make it."

"No. No. It's no use," Quartz replied feebly, coughing, and a trickle of blood came from the corner of his mouth and ran down his chin.

"You know, maybe you're right, Dan," the minister said, and he coughed again. "Maybe you were the instrument that the Almighty sent to mete out vengeance."

"I'll get the other two, Eli, I promise you," Drage said softly.

Quartz smiled at him. Then he coughed, and his body jerked spasmodically, then went still. Dan Drage reached over and gently closed the minister's eyes. He very carefully and slowly lowered Eli Quartz's head down to the floor of the church aisle.

There were tears in the dark eyes of the lanky gunslinger as he looked down upon his friend's body.

XII

Two men from the town rushed into the church then, through the front door. They had heard the shots and had come to investigate. They started down the aisle toward the man on the floor. Then they saw what had happened and they stopped, swept their hats off in deference to the minister, and stood awkwardly in the aisle.

"Will you two see that the minister's

body is properly taken care of?" Drage asked them.

"Yes, sir, we sure will," one of them said.

"He was a fine man," the other said.

Drage indicated the body of Frank Gideon lying there.

"See that that piece of garbage is cleaned up, too," he said.

"Right. We'll do that."

Drage turned and rushed up the aisle and out the front door. He ran down the church steps and headed down the street, back toward the bank. He quickly grabbed his horse's reins and swung up into the saddle.

There were some men who had gathered outside of the bank and Drage asked them:

"Did you see which way they went?"

"That way," one of the men said, pointing down the road that led south out of town.

Drage nodded, murmured his thanks, and urged his horse into motion. His face was grim as he rode. He had no way of being sure where the two other Gideon brothers were headed. But he did know the direction they were going and he did know that he was not far behind them.

He had killed one of the three brothers he had been chasing. However, he was well aware that he had paid a bitter price for being able to get just one of them. His friend of many years, Eli Quartz, was dead. So was the sheriff. This was added to the deaths of his brother and his brother's wife and it gave him more reason to keep after the two men.

It might be, Drage mused as he rode, that vengeance was in the hands of the Almighty. But now, with this latest death to avenge, Dan Drage felt that it was his calling in life, even more than he had felt it before, to be one of the instruments of that eternal vengeance.

He was constantly alert as he rode. His dark eyes scanned the nearby rocks, the bushes, and the ravines on the nearby hills. He did not want to be surprised or ambushed by the two Gideons. He thought that they would probably be running and running hard instead of waiting to bushwhack anyone. But he could not afford the luxury of letting down his guard.

It was a late August day and the sun was very hot. Heat waves shimmered up from the desert floor and created mirages and images that could trick a man into believing there were men hiding where there really were none.

Dan Drage, having lived in a desert area, was used to these images. In addition to being aware of the tricks of nature, he was well aware of the machinations of men. And men had a way of being unpredictable. Drage knew it was smart to be prepared for anything at any time.

So he never let himself become complacent. He practiced with his revolver constantly. He knew that he could not afford to let himself slow down. All the same, at some time there would come someone who was just a fraction of a second faster, perhaps just a shade more accurate, and then Dan Drage would be no more.

Would his nemesis be one of the two Gideon brothers?

XIII

When Walt and Tubby Gideon left their brother Frank at the bank and galloped out of town, they each took separate roads. But, as soon as they had passed the outbuildings of the town, they managed to get back together again and, side by side, they charged down the main road that led to the south.

"What happened to Frank?" Walt called out to his brother.

"They shot his horse out from under him," Tubby yelled back at Walt. "He got off and was running away down the street, but I didn't see him after that. I don't know if they got him or not."

Walt swore. "I hope he gets away," he yelled. "But we can't take the time to go back for him now. By this time the whole town will be swarming with people toting guns."

Tubby looked back over his shoulder as they rode.

"I don't think there's anybody after us," he called. "At least I don't see them."

Walt grinned at his brother.

"I told you so," he said. "Without their sheriff, these little towns are completely helpless. There just ain't nobody there who has the guts to form a posse."

They rode hard for a short time and then finally slowed down so that their horses would not be overtired. Continuing down the road, they came to a small side road that led to the west, into a canyon that ran between two hills. A weathered gray wooden sign, which was nailed to a post at the side of the road, declared that this was the road that led to the MS Ranch.

"Hey!" Walt said, reining his horse to a stop. "This is our answer. We'll go up this road to that ranch and we'll just hole up there for a couple of days. After that we can ride on without any concern."

"But what about Frank?" the ever-nervous Tubby asked. "How will he be able to find us if we're holed up at one of the local ranches? He won't know where we are."

"How will he find us anyway if we keep pounding down this road?" Walt retorted. "We'll get hooked back up with him down in New Mexico, *if* he ever makes it out of the town of Helaman."

"But how do we know who'll be at this ranch down here?" Tubby went on, his fears growing worse. "How do we dare just ride in there?"

"We won't just ride in there," Walt said, forcing himself to be patient although he was getting irritated with his brother. "We'll ride in from the side of the ranch and just look the place over. If there's too

much activity going on there, maybe we'll
just hide out in one of their sheds or barns
or something."

So the two of them turned off the main
roadway and guided their horses along
the side road that led between the two
hills. As they neared the ranch, they
moved off the road into the brush on one
hillside. When Walt and Tubby got fairly
close to the ranch buildings themselves,
they got off their horses, tied them to some
oak brush, and crept over to where they
could see down in the small saucer-shaped
valley below.

The area around the house was green
with the lush grass of late summer. There
was a barn, a corral, and a few outbuildings. The place was definitely kept up, as
evidenced by the whitewashed buildings
and the small cultivated garden off to one
side of the house.

After the men had watched the place
for some time, Tubby said:

"It looks like it's a fairly small spread."

"Yeah, it does at that," Walt agreed.
"And while we've been watching it here,
I've only seen one old man and one woman

around the place. There might be more
hands out on the range or someplace else,
of course, but it looks like those two are
the only ones around the ranch house.
Seems like a small operation."

"What shall we do?" Tubby asked, waiting as usual for Walt to make a decision.

"Well, I think we'll just go down and
pay those folks a visit," Walt said almost
jovially. "We'll tell them we'll be staying
with them for a little while."

Tubby laughed. "Yeah. We'll tell them
we've come to pay them a neighborly
visit."

So the two of them led their horses down
the slope, keeping the large white barn
between them and the house at all times.
This prevented anyone in the house from
seeing them as they came down the hill.

They tethered their horses behind the
barn and, with drawn six-guns, the two
Gideon brothers crept cautiously around
the barn.

The older man was working in the yard
in back of the house. He was not wearing
a gun and the two newcomers moved up
to him silently. They were only a few yards

away when he looked up and saw them.

"What the—!" he began.

"Hold it," Walt Gideon told him. "Don't make any funny moves or you're dead!"

"What do you want? What are you men doing here?" the older man asked.

"We're just friendly fellows who want to stay and visit with you for a while," Walt said. "Now let's go into the house."

He motioned with his revolver and the other man knew that he meant business. The older man did not want to submit to their demands, but he had no choice. Slowly and sullenly he led the two gunmen to the back door of the house.

Near the door, Walt Gideon moved to the front of the line. He quietly opened the door.

Marie Sandoval was in the kitchen and turned, suddenly startled, to face the six-gun in the hand of Walt Gideon. She looked around her in the kitchen, her eyes rapidly searching for a gun, a knife, or some other weapon with which to defend herself.

Walt raised the muzzle of the gun so that it pointed at her face.

"Don't even think about trying any-thing, lady," he warned her as he saw her look about hastily. "I've killed before and I would just as soon shoot you as not. Don't give me any excuse."

They ushered the older man into the kitchen then and the four of them crowded into the small room.

"Elmer," the woman said, "have they hurt you?"

"Nobody's been hurt yet," Walt Gideon said, "and they won't be hurt if you just cooperate."

"I know who you are," Marie Sandoval said as the realization struck her. "You're the man who killed Sheriff Nielsen."

"You got it right, lady," Tubby said. "And we ain't afraid to kill again."

"Shut up," Walt told Tubby. "You talk too much." He had not yet decided what they were going to do with the woman and her old hired hand, but he saw no need to tell them too much and to advertise all their previous deeds.

"Let's go out into the front room," Walt Gideon said, "where we can all be more comfortable together."

XIV

The four of them went through the connecting door into the parlor of the house. Marie Sandoval and Elmer sat down on the couch together, and Walt and Tubby Gideon pulled up two separate chairs and sat down facing the couch.

"All right, here's what the deal is," Walt Gideon told them. "We need a place to hide out for a couple of days until the dust settles down in the town of Helaman and people quit looking for us. As soon as things are quiet around here, then we'll just ride on and let you alone."

"Leaving us dead, no doubt," Marie Sandoval said, her dark eyes flashing.

"Now, ma'am, it doesn't have to be that way," Walt Gideon said. "I'm willing to live and let live. You just have to be sure that you don't try to get away or do anything, and my brother and I will move on without any fuss."

Marie Sandoval looked at Walt and said nothing. She didn't want to promise that she would not try to get away because she knew that she would if she could. On the other hand, she didn't want to throw idle threats at the man either. She did not want to anger him and cause him to shoot her right here and now.

She had no illusions, however, that these two gunmen would merely leave them alone and ride on their way after this was all over. These were wicked men, and killing her and Elmer would be of no moral concern to them. Human life was obviously cheap to them.

"All right now, Elmer," Walt went on,

"you go out in the kitchen and hustle us all up some grub. Leave the door open between the rooms, and remember that if you try anything, Miss Sandoval here is likely to die."

Elmer glared at Walt and reluctantly got to his feet. He would have liked to jump them right here and now, in spite of the consequences, but he had a fierce loyalty to Marie Sandoval and he would not do anything that would jeopardize her safety. And so he moved toward the kitchen to do as he was told by Walt Gideon.

"Tubby," Walt went on, "you go out and unsaddle our horses. Put them in the corral there behind the barn. And then be sure to bring the saddlebags in the house with you."

The saddlebags contained the money that they had stolen from the bank. Walt Gideon was not about to leave those bags outside where anyone might get hold of them. He wanted them inside, and close by, where he could keep an eye on them.

"Why me?" Tubby complained. "Why do I have to go out and do it?"

"Because I said so!" Walt told him, and there was no arguing with the commanding tone of his voice. He was fully in charge now and he would brook no arguments from anyone, especially his weaker brother. "I'm going to stay here with the lovely Miss Sandoval," he continued with a leer, "just to make sure that she doesn't go anyplace or get any fancy ideas about trying to bushwhack us."

Marie Sandoval bristled and glared at Walt Gideon, but she continued to say nothing.

Mumbling mostly to himself, but also for the benefit of his audience, that he was the one who had to do all of the dirty work, Tubby got to his feet. He stomped through the kitchen and out the back door of the house.

Marie Sandoval told herself that she must be very careful what she said to these men. She must not antagonize them by taunting them. Also, she must be careful that she did not mention, or even allude to, the fact that they were probably being followed by Dan Drage. She didn't know if they were even aware Dan Drage was

in the area. However, she was sure that
Drage was after them.

Even as Marie sat in the room with Walt
Gideon and contemplated these things,
Dan Drage was riding south along the
main roadway leading out of Helaman.
He was still watching the surrounding
countryside for the men he was pursuing
and searching for the prints of horses'
hooves in the gray Colorado dust.

He was sure that he saw hoofprints in
the road from time to time. He was not
sure that those prints were made by the
horses of the men he sought. But there
was a good chance they were.

Dan suddenly came to the small side
road that went west, the road with the
weathered sign that pointed to the MS
Ranch.

"MS," Drage mused aloud. "Must be the
ranch that belongs to Marie Sandoval.
Hmmm."

He studied the side road and could see
the distinct prints of the hooves of two
horses in the dirt. Most probably the two
Gideon brothers had turned off the main
road and had headed toward the Sandoval

ranch. In fact, if Drage had been them and
had been fleeing from town after a robbery, that was exactly what he would have
done too.

Drage did not believe that the two Gideons could be very far ahead of him. Even
taking into account the time that he had
spent hunting down Frank Gideon, he
could not be far behind the remaining
brothers.

He turned his horse onto the side road
that led toward the ranch. After riding a
short distance, he left the road and moved
into the brush. He did not know where
the Sandoval ranch was located exactly,
and decided to approach it cautiously.
Then he saw it appear below him quite
unexpectedly.

Tubby Gideon had taken the saddles off
the two horses and had put the horses in
the corral. He had removed the saddlebags and was headed back toward the
house with those saddlebags when he
looked up toward the nearby hill and saw,
in the distance, a tall rider seated on a
black horse.

Tubby did not go for his gun or make any other sudden moves that would alert the rider to the fact that he had been spotted. Tubby merely kept walking at the same pace toward the house with the saddlebags slung over his shoulder.

Dan Drage saw the man in the distance walking from the corral to the ranch house. But because Tubby Gideon was discreet, Drage did not know that the man had spotted him.

Tubby kept moving toward the back door of the well-kept ranch house as though he had all day and there wasn't another person for miles around.

Drage sat his horse for a while longer and watched the scene below. Then he moved deeper into some brush where he couldn't be seen from below. And he began to work himself closer to the house.

XV

Tubby Gideon brought the saddlebags
into the front room where Marie Sandoval, Walt Gideon, and Elmer were
drinking the coffee and eating the fried
potatoes that Elmer had prepared. Tubby
dropped the bags at Walt's feet and then
picked up a cup of coffee. He sat down in
a chair and started sipping the coffee.

Marie Sandoval looked at the saddlebags and the canvas bank bag that was

slipping out of one bag.

"That's one of the bags from the Wells Fargo Bank," she said. "So, that's your game. You've killed the sheriff, and now you've robbed the bank!"

Walt laughed. "Well, how did you think we were making a living? There might be a lot of satisfaction in killing sheriffs, but it don't buy any beans and bacon. Sure, we robbed the bank. What are you going to do about it, little lady?"

She bit her lip and didn't respond. One word from her, and they might start shooting.

Tubby was smiling at Marie's discomfiture and the way his brother was baiting her. In fact, he had almost forgotten the thing that he needed to tell Walt. He took one of the pieces of potato in his mouth, chewed it, and washed it down with a swallow of coffee.

Then he said, almost as though he were making casual conversation:

"When I was outside just now, I saw a rider up on the rise to the north of the ranch."

"A rider!" Walt exploded. "Why didn't you say something about it before now? Was he there alone? Did he look like a lawman? What was he doing?"

Tubby was amused that he had been able to get his brother's goat so easily. He was not often able to best his brother in anything. It gave Tubby a bit of a feeling of superiority for one of the few times in his life and he enjoyed it.

"Far as I could see, the man was alone," Tubby finally drawled, drawing out his enjoyment. "I couldn't see no star on his chest, but then he was a fair distance away from me, so I don't know if I could have seen a badge or not. From where I was looking, he didn't particularly look like a lawman."

"Lawmen don't all have to look alike," Walt sneered sarcastically. "He didn't have to *look* like a lawman to be a lawman. They don't need to advertise."

Walt sat for a moment, thinking about the implications of what his brother had seen. He sipped some of the dark, hot, bitter coffee.

Then he said:

"There was just one man up on the hill, huh?"

"Yeah," Tubby answered, obviously unperturbed and still enjoying himself since he saw that he had his brother's attention. "The man was alone."

Walt got up from his chair and paced the floor. He looked out the window although he didn't expect to see anything or anyone. Then he turned back to Marie.

"Are there any other ranches close to here?" he asked her.

She shook her head. "No, there aren't," she said.

She thought that it was best to be honest with the man. She didn't know how much he knew about the area and whether he was just testing her. If the two of them had ridden around here much, they would probably be aware that her ranch was the only one in this particular area. If she lied to them, she might just anger them—and earn a fatal bullet.

She had thought, from the moment that Tubby spoke up about seeing the rider, that the man was probably Dan Drage.

However, she thought that it would be well if the Gideon brothers did not suspect anything.

So she went on:

"It isn't unusual for people to be riding around this area. Oftentimes, riders pass close by to this place. We aren't too far from the main trail out of Helaman."

Marie realized that she might be spreading it on a little too thick. In her desire to lead them away from any possible suspicion of Dan Drage or anyone who might be following them, she didn't want to say so much that they would suspect her of covering up for someone. So she said no more.

Walt looked at her suspiciously. "Yeah. Maybe," he said in response.

He put his coffee cup down and slid his long-barreled revolver out of its holster. He spun the cylinder automatically, checking to make sure it was loaded, although he knew that he had reloaded it after firing it.

Then Walt turned to Tubby and said:

"I'm going outside. You get your six-gun in your hand and you hold it on these two. Don't let them try anything. I don't want them to get away with a thing. Do you understand?"

Walt was being domineering and demanding again. Tubby had lost the advantage he had had in dealing with his brother.

"I don't think that rider I saw was anybody to get excited about," Tubby said, trying to regain his edge.

"I, personally, don't think that we can trust *anybody*," Walt said, waving his six-gun for emphasis. "Now I'm going out there and check on what's happening. You keep control of things in here, if you think you can."

The last was said sarcastically, and Tubby did not appreciate the tone of his brother's voice. Walt turned and walked out of the front room, through the kitchen, and out the back door. He looked carefully to the right and to the left. Seeing no one, he slowly moved a bit further.

The afternoon sun burned brightly. Walt took a deep breath and started walking in the direction of the whitewashed barn.

XVI

Standing behind a group of dark-green scrub oak, Dan Drage watched Walt Gideon walk from the house. Drage had dismounted from his horse earlier and left it tethered in a secluded spot where it could not be seen from the yard.

Drage knew that the man he was watching was Walt Gideon. He had carefully studied the wanted posters and some old photographs so that he could clearly identify each of the Gideon brothers.

Drage also knew that he could probably gun Walt down from where he stood, even though it was some distance away. However, he did not know what was happening inside the house and where Tubby was and what he was doing. And Drage was not about to endanger the life of Marie Sandoval or any other innocent bystander if he could help it.

So Dan carefully made his way back up to his horse and led it down toward the barn. But by now he had lost track of Walt Gideon. He assumed, though, that the man had gone into the barn, since that was the way he'd been headed.

Drage slowly moved toward the barn. As he reached the back of the large, whitewashed building, he let go of the horse's reins and just let it wander. He knew that the well-trained animal would not stray far from the ranch buildings.

Now Drage slowly drew the Colt .44 from its low-slung holster. Holding the revolver in front of him with the barrel slightly elevated, he cautiously worked his way around the building, being on the alert for any sign of the other man.

As he came around the front corner of the building, he could see that the large door of the barn was slightly ajar. Drage flattened himself against the building and made his way toward the open door.

Unfortunately, Drage was too sure that Walt had gone into the barn. He did not check all the other possible hiding places.

So he did not spot Walt Gideon, who was concealed behind a wagon that was standing about halfway between the house and the barn. The wagon had been there for some time and the weeds had grown up around its wheels, so anyone looking at it could not see under it.

Walt Gideon had fooled Drage just as he had hoped to. Drage was coming around the barn with his attention riveted on the barn door, assuming that Gideon had gone inside. Drage was paying almost no heed to anyplace else, just the barn door.

Now he was just preparing to slip inside the barn.

Walt Gideon, from his hiding place behind the wagon, was watching Drage closely, following him with the long barrel of his revolver. But just as he began to squeeze the trigger, he bumped into the wagon wheel. And that was just enough to throw his aim off slightly. The large six-gun roared ominously, but the bullet merely plucked at Dan Drage's sleeve.

Drage immediately threw himself to the ground and sent a shot toward the wagon, then quickly crawled the short distance to the relative safety of the barn.

Dan's shot at Walt Gideon also went wild, hitting the wagon bed and throwing wooden splinters into Gideon's face.

Gideon recovered quickly and fired back at the barn door, but it was mainly to keep the man inside the barn. Walt knew that he wouldn't be able to hit him because the man was now out of sight.

Walt Gideon had no idea whom his adversary was. The man was not wearing a star, as far as Gideon had been able to tell, so Walt supposed that he was not a lawman. Also, the stranger seemed to be alone, so there was no posse involved.

It could be, Walt Gideon thought to himself as he hunched behind the wagon, that the man in the barn was just a drifter, one of the many saddle tramps who frequented the area, perhaps a man who had just stopped by to steal what he could from the ranch on his way to someplace else.

But whoever or whatever the man was, Walt Gideon knew that he could not afford to take chances. It could be someone who was after him and Tubby. And Gideon felt that he had to take care of the man in the barn, and take care of him permanently.

Walt slowly rose from his crouched position. He kept his pistol leveled at the barn door in case the man reappeared. Walt Gideon had no intention of going into the barn after the gunslinger. That would be a way to get ambushed. Eventually, the stranger would have to leave the barn from the front door or the back.

There was a small clump of scrub oak facing the side of the barn, and Gideon carefully edged his way behind that. He now had a good view of both the front and back doors of the barn.

Walt kept his pistol ready so he could use it immediately if he needed to and just settled down to wait, hoping that the wiry

stranger would come out of the barn
quickly. Then Gideon would be able to get
him.

Dan Drage crouched in the barn. He
had watched Walt Gideon through a crack
between the wooden boards of the building. He knew exactly where Gideon was.
Drage even thought that he might be able
to shoot the man from where he was in
the barn. But, again, he had to be concerned about what might happen to the
people inside the house if he were to kill
Walt Gideon out here in the yard.

He assumed that Tubby Gideon had
Marie Sandoval inside captive, along with
whoever else might have been around
when the two brothers rode in. No, Dan
did not dare make too rash a move.

He knew the Gideons were a trigger-
happy clan, and he must see to it that no
triggers were needlessly fired.

XVII

Inside the house, Tubby Gideon was becoming nervous. Time after time, he wiped his sweating forehead with his sleeve. The gunshots he had heard outside had put him on edge, and Marie Sandoval's words added to his anxiety.

"They've probably killed your brother outside there," she said in a taunting tone.

"They ain't killed Walt!" Tubby replied

vehemently. "They ain't never going to kill Walt!"

"Maybe the house is surrounded by an armed posse," Marie went on.

She wasn't as afraid of Tubby as she was of Walt. She perceived that Tubby was the more vulnerable and she thought she could get away with goading him. She hoped she was right.

"There ain't no posse out there!" Tubby exclaimed. "There's only one man."

"Perhaps you only saw one," she said. "That doesn't mean there weren't more hiding back behind the hills."

Tubby's gun hand had begun to tremble as she talked, and he tried to steady it.

"You just shut up!" he yelled at her. "You quit talking like that or I'm going to shoot you! I'll shoot you like Walt did that tin-badge sheriff in town."

Marie Sandoval realized that she was probably going too far at this point. Although Tubby was the weaker of the brothers, he could still be very dangerous. His nervousness or fear might cause him to shoot her.

Tubby paced the room now, waving his six-gun around and ranting and raving. Marie Sandoval became subdued, just watching and waiting.

Finally, Tubby's nervousness and apprehension got the better of him. He did what he knew his brother Walt would not have wanted him to do. He walked through the small kitchen and stood in the open doorway, glancing out.

He looked all around him and then yelled:

"Walt! Walt! I heard shots out here. Are you okay, Walt?"

Walt Gideon, hidden in the small stand of oak brush, did not immediately answer, trying not to call attention to himself, trying to stay hidden from the tall stranger who was still in the barn.

Tubby stepped out the back door then and into the backyard. Total panic had overcome him by now and he was waving the six-gun around.

"Walt! Walt! Where are you? Are you all right, Walt?" he called out.

"I'm over here, you damn fool!" Walt finally yelled at his brother, the exasperation evident in his voice.

Still keeping a wary eye on the barn doors, front and back, Walt moved out of the scrub-oak patch and looked toward the house where Tubby was standing.

"Get back in that house!" Walt yelled at his brother. "You're supposed to be keeping an eye on the woman and the old man! I'll take care of things out here. You do what you're supposed to."

Meanwhile, Elmer had gotten up from his chair and moved through the kitchen following Tubby. As Tubby stepped out the back door, Elmer quietly took a large butcher knife from one of the drawers in the kitchen cabinet.

As the two brothers were yelling at each other, Elmer slowly raised the knife and stealthily moved toward Tubby.

Just then Walt Gideon told Tubby to get back in the house.

Tubby started to turn while Elmer brought the knife down in a vicious thrust. Seeing the danger in time, Tubby was able to escape lightly. The flashing knife slashed down, slitting the left sleeve of Tubby's shirt. The knife also cut the man's arm open. It wasn't a deep cut, though. But it was a long slash, running the length of the arm. Blood immediately oozed from the gash and Tubby Gideon felt the sharp pain of the knife.

Tubby yelled and swung his six-gun around with his right hand, trying to get at the man who had attacked him with the knife. By that time, Marie Sandoval had left the front room and come to the kitchen.

Without thinking, the young woman grabbed for the arm with the gun. Then Marie Sandoval and Elmer were both grappling with Tubby. Elmer still had the large butcher knife in his hand and was trying to bury it in Tubby's chest. Tubby still had his six-gun in his right hand and was trying to fire at one or both of his attackers.

From his vantage point in the middle of the dark-green scrub-oak stand, Walt Gideon saw what was happening at the back door of the house. In his concern for the safety of his brother, Walt forgot entirely about the man in the barn. He stepped out of the oak brush and started to run toward the house.

Walt had his revolver in his hand, but he could not use it for fear of hitting Tubby. He would have liked to shoot at the woman or the old man, but he didn't dare do so, since the three of them were struggling together and he could not get a clear shot.

From where he was crouched down in the barn, looking between the wooden boards, Dan Drage could not see what was going on at the back of the house. He had heard Walt and Tubby yelling at each other. Then he heard the sounds of the scuffle at the house. Finally, he saw Walt leave the oak brush and run toward the house. But he could not actually see the house.

Taking advantage of Walt's departure, Drage quickly ran from the barn door.

As he ran, he glanced over at the house. He saw the three people fighting and he could see Walt Gideon running toward them.

Drage would have fired in an attempt to kill one of the Gideon brothers, but he was fearful of hitting Marie Sandoval or the old man. He thought of running toward the group struggling at the house, but he was afraid that such a move might make one of the Gideon brothers shoot their two struggling captives.

Instead of moving toward the house, Drage ran away from it, hiding behind a large rock out in the field.

Panting from his running, Drage slowly drew his Colt. And he waited.

XVIII

When Walt Gideon reached the three
people who were engaged in a life-and-
death struggle by the house, he raised his
gun and clubbed Marie Sandoval with the
butt.

He did not hit her hard, but it was hard
enough to have the desired effect. Marie
staggered back and let go of Tubby's gun
hand.

With his hand free, Tubby immediately

123

aimed the gun at Elmer, who was lunging at him with the butcher knife, not wounding him seriously but inflicting several small cuts on Tubby's arms and chest.

The six-gun roared and the older man gasped. A look of disbelief crossed his face as the pain and shock went through him. Suddenly, Elmer relaxed his grip and the knife clattered to the ground.

Elmer grabbed at his abdomen. An agonized look was on his face as he crumpled and fell down.

"Elmer!" Marie Sandoval screamed.

She rushed to crouch by the old man's side, putting the palm of her hand on his cheek and trying to comfort him.

Tubby Gideon stepped back and shoved his six-gun into its holster. He took the bandana from around his neck and began dabbing at the long cut down his arm, which was bleeding.

"Come on. Let's all get into the house," Walt Gideon said gruffly, gesturing with the six-gun that was still in his right hand.

He glanced back at the barn with its door still ajar. He seemed to be aware for the first time that he had left the wiry stranger unattended. Now he was not at all sure whether the man was still in the barn. In fact, Walt was afraid that he had lost his quarry.

"I'm bleeding!" Tubby wailed as Walt ushered him into the house.

"So what?" Walt responded. "You ain't hurt that much. You ain't going to die. Just get in the house, get out of sight."

Tubby did as he was told. He shuffled through the doorway. Walt bent down and prodded the kneeling Marie Sandoval with the barrel of his gun.

"Get up and get on into the house," he told her.

Marie looked up, hatred masking the otherwise beautiful features of her face.

"You've killed Elmer!" she said.

"It was his own fault," Walt said. "He shouldn't have come charging out here with that knife and tried to kill Tubby. It was his own fault," he repeated. "Anyway, Tubby did it."

"But he was an old man," she protested. "You didn't need to kill him."

"Look, lady, he ain't the first one we've killed, and he ain't likely to be the last.

Now you get up and get into the house or you might be the next one to be shot."

There was no mistaking the seriousness of his voice. Marie Sandoval felt nothing but hatred and disgust for the man, but she knew she had better do as she was told.

She reluctantly got up and left Elmer's body and walked through the back door of the house. Tubby was in the front room, still complaining and still trying—with the bandana—to stop the blood now coming more slowly from the cut on his arm.

Walt Gideon looked about the ranch yard. He stared at the barn for a long time, but there was no sign of anyone around and there was no movement. He shoved his six-gun into its holster, bent down, and took hold of the upper arms of the dead man.

Gideon dragged Elmer's body over to a small storage shed by a corner of the house, opened the door, shoved the body inside on top of some boxes, and then shut the shed door.

Walt went back into the house and into the well-kept front room where Marie and

Tubby were sitting, eyeing each other with thinly veiled antagonism. Walt sat down in one of the chairs and Tubby looked at him.

"What were the shots out there before?" Tubby asked. "What was happening to you?"

"I went out and spotted that wrangler you saw up on the hill," Walt replied. "I took a couple of shots at him and chased him into the barn."

"Is he still out there?" Tubby asked, still dabbing at his left arm with the bandana.

"I don't know," Walt responded, a note of annoyance in his voice. "When you came whooping and hollering outside and then the old man jumped you, I had to come to your rescue, if you remember. The gunslinger might have gotten away by now. He may be halfway to New Mexico for all I know."

The sarcasm was largely lost on Tubby. He did not believe that he was at fault. He had been concerned about Walt, so he had gone outside and called to him. It still seemed like the right thing to have done. The fact that Elmer had come out and jumped him with the knife was a totally unrelated circumstance, as far as Tubby was concerned.

"Do we dare just sit in here and do nothing? What if he's still out there?" Tubby asked.

Walt glared at him. He hated it when his younger brother questioned him or challenged him—especially when Tubby was right.

"No," Walt snapped, "we're not going to just sit in here and wait for him to take potshots at us. We're going out after him. It's just that I had to save your neck first."

That made Walt feel better. He had laid the blame on Tubby. It wasn't his fault that he had been unable to gun down the unknown stranger.

Walt Gideon turned and looked at Marie Sandoval, who was sitting on the couch, pale and drawn from the ordeal with Elmer. She had said nothing; she was thinking about her old friend lying outside.

Gideon pulled his revolver as he looked at her. It was obvious that he was thinking about Marie and wondering what to do with her. Tubby sensed that Walt was thinking about that and he voiced the question that was already in Walt's mind.

"What about her?"

As much crime as Walt Gideon had been involved in, and as cruel and merciless as he had become over the past years, he was still not totally callous. He did not like to think about killing women. He had shot that woman at the bank robbery up in Cheyenne, Wyoming, but that had been when they were trying to make their getaway and he was shooting at anything that moved. He had also threatened to shoot Marie Sandoval just now outside of the house. But that was just a threat and the shooting in Cheyenne was just a fluke. Walt didn't ordinarily do that and he would not just kill a woman in cold blood if he could possibly avoid it.

"We'll just tie her up," Walt finally decided, "and keep her here—all tied up— while we go out and take care of that saddle tramp."

"Do you think that's all he is," Tubby asked, "a saddle tramp?"

"I think so," Walt said, his confidence returning. "But we'd better get rid of him anyway. He's seen me and I've taken a shot at him, so he'll be better off out of the way."

Then Walt turned to Marie Sandoval.

"Where's some rope?" he asked her.

She was about to give him some acid comment just to show her bravado and her disgust at him, but then she thought better of it. She felt that she had probably just been saved from immediate death at the hands of these men, so she decided that she had better play along with them and not do anything else to anger them.

"There is some clothesline rope in the small cupboard out in the kitchen," she sullenly told Walt Gideon.

Tubby got up after a look from Walt, went out of the room, and, in a few minutes, brought back a coil of rope. As Walt watched with his gun still trained on the woman, Tubby trussed Marie up, tying the knots none too gently. He secured her arms behind the chair and then he roped her legs to the chair legs.

When Tubby had finished the job, Walt tested the knots. Apparently, they were tied to his satisfaction. The two of them

left the room and went into the kitchen
and stood at the back door.

"All right," Walt said to his brother,
"when we go out to the barn, you go first
and I'll cover you from here. Don't go inside the barn. Just stand to the side of the
door. Then you cover me and I'll follow
you out there. After we get to the barn,
we'll see if he's still inside."

"Why do I have to go first?" Tubby
whined.

Walt tried to be patient. When he ad-
dressed his brother, he sounded as if he
were talking to a slightly retarded child.

"Because somebody has to go first and
it might as well be you. I made the decision. Now just do what you're told!"

XIX

During the time that the Gideons had
been tying up Marie Sandoval, Dan Drage
had been slowly working his way toward
the house. He kept behind rocks, trees,
and bushes and made sure that he could
not be seen from any of the windows of
the house, in case someone was looking
out.

He was crouched in a clump of the

133

dark-green scrub oak that dotted the area when he saw the back door open again.

Drage crouched even lower in the brush and held his Colt .44 at the ready. As he watched, Tubby Gideon came out and crossed quickly to the barn. As soon as Tubby had reached the barn, Walt Gideon crossed over to him.

Drage could have shot one of them, but he feared the other might be able to take revenge against the people in the house. So he merely held his six-gun and watched the two men.

"You stand here at the side of the door where you can see inside," Walt told Tubby. "You cover me and I'll go inside."

Gingerly and stealthily Walt walked into the dim light of the barn, swinging his six-gun back and forth in front of him as though to cover the entire interior of the structure. His nerves were taut and his senses were alert.

Tubby stood at the corner of the doorway and alternately looked inside at Walt and outside at the surrounding area.

Drage knew that he could get Tubby without any problem. His concern was

what happened after that. He still had the
same dilemma which had presented itself
to him ever since he came to the ranch
and realized that the two brothers had
taken Marie Sandoval and perhaps others
hostage. He was sure that Marie Sandoval was inside the house, but he was
not aware of where anyone else might be.
He did not see the outcome of the fight
between Elmer and Tubby, and he had no
idea where other innocent people from the
ranch might be hiding. He did not want
to harm any of them.

As Drage watched, and Tubby stood
guard outside of the barn door, Walt Gideon started to climb the ladder from the
floor of the barn up to the hayloft.

He was only a few feet up when his foot
slipped off a rung of the ladder. He swore
and fell the few feet to the ground. Tubby
could not see what was happening and he
threw the door open and rushed inside the
barn.

"Walt! Walt! Are you all right?" he
yelled, the ever-present fear in his voice.

As soon as Tubby disappeared into the
barn, Dan Drage ran as hard as he could

to the front of the house. He tried the knob on the front door. It turned easily, and he slipped inside the house.

Marie Sandoval was sitting tied to a chair in the front room. She looked up. At first her expression was fearful since she did not know what to expect or who might be coming in. Then she recognized him and obvious relief flooded her face.

"Oh," she said, "thank heaven you're here."

Drage looked around to make sure that there was no one else in the room. Then he quickly untied the ropes. She stood up and rubbed her wrists to ease the pain that had been caused by the binding ropes.

"We have to get you out of the house right now," Dan said.

"Aren't you going to fight them?" she asked. "Aren't you going to take care of them for what they've done? They killed the sheriff and they killed my hired man, Elmer."

"I am sorry about that," he told her. "But I want to face them on our terms, not on theirs. And if there is going to be shooting, I certainly don't want it taking

place while you're right here in the line
of fire."

"Then what are we going to do?" she
asked him, putting herself at his command.

"I saw a little cave up on the nearby
hill," he said. "If we can get to that and
hole up in it for a while, then we can come
down and deal with them in our own time
and on the terms we dictate."

"Yes," she responded. "It's a small cave
that we once used for storage. We don't
use it anymore. There'll be room enough
for both of us to get in there. I just don't
like the idea of hiding from these men."

"It will just be a while," he promised
her.

He looked around the room and eyed
the saddlebags sitting by the couch. He
realized immediately that was where the
money from the bank was hidden. She
saw the direction of his glance.

"They robbed the bank," she said.

"I know," he answered, "and killed Eli
Quartz in the bargain."

Her hand went to her mouth in a
shocked expression.

"Oh, no," she said softly, "not the minister."

"That's one more score I have to settle," he said. "But come on. Now we have to go." And he took her arm and guided her toward the front door.

"I have to get my rifle," she said. "I may need that."

"You may at that," he agreed.

He grabbed the Winchester .76 from its rack above the fireplace, handed it to her, and the two of them went quickly out of the house.

XX

Walt and Tubby Gideon walked out of the barn with their pistols still in their hands, ready for action. They had thoroughly searched the place and had not found the man they were looking for. Walt had been scolding Tubby for not staying at his post outside the barn, but it didn't matter. That was all behind them now.

They started walking back toward the house together when suddenly Tubby looked up and pointed.

"Look," he said, excitement in his voice. "There's the man and the woman going up that hill. Look over there!"

Walt looked up and saw the two. And immediately he dropped to his knee and raised his six-gun. Aiming carefully, he squeezed the trigger.

The revolver roared and spit flame, and the bullet hit the dirt just behind Dan Drage and Marie Sandoval.

Marie flinched and stumbled at the sound of the shooting. Drage looked quickly at her, a momentary fear coming over him. Then he saw that she wasn't hit. He grabbed her arm tightly with his right hand and half-pulled, half-lifted her farther up the hill.

"Come on," he said to her urgently, "we have to keep moving so they can't get a good aim on us."

As he half-pulled, half-carried her along, Marie was impressed by the strength of this man. Although his outward appearance gave one the impression that he was nothing but skin and bones, he was obviously very muscular. He seemed able to do anything physical that was required of him.

As they continued moving up the hill, there were two more shots from the Gideons. One bullet kicked up dirt at the side of them and the other one whined over their heads.

As they ran, Drage jerked Marie first to one side and then the other to throw off the aim of their adversaries below them. And the Gideons' next two shots went wild.

"We're almost out of range of their guns," Dan told her. "Let's hurry."

Before long the two of them reached the small cave.

Drage had to stoop down to enter the mouth of the cavern. And it was only about twelve feet from the cave entrance to the back wall.

"This isn't hardly big enough to keep a herd of fleas in," Drage remarked, "but I think it's probably big enough for what we need."

They went all the way into the cave and Marie sat down on the floor with her back against the rear wall. She stared at Drage and smiled wistfully.

"We used to come up here and play in this cave when we were younger," she said. "It was just the right size for us then, just right for children."

"We?" he asked.

"My brother and I," Marie answered him. "My mother, father, brother, and I moved out here when I was eight years old. Mother and Father have died since then and my brother went off to fight in the Civil War."

"And?" he prodded.

"We've never heard from him since. After the War, I wrote to the War Department and everyone I could think of to find out what had happened to him. But no one really knew. Finally, they listed him as—as 'missing in action.' I guess, whether I want to or not, I have to assume he's dead."

"I'm very sorry," Drage told her sincerely.

As they went on talking, Marie could see that he was busy at the mouth of the cave. He was arranging branches and dried leaves in a tight semicircle around the entrance. He fixed the brush so that he could see beyond it and it did not obstruct his view.

"What are you doing?" Marie asked inquisitively.

"I'm putting this dried brush out here in case someone tries to sneak up on us in the night. It makes a good watchman. It crackles when you step on it. It is getting dark, you noticed."

"Yes," she said, and some fear showed in her face and voice. "I know that it's getting on to nighttime. I've been a little worried about that, with those two men down there who are apt to come up here after us."

"That's what the dried brush is for," he reminded her, "just in case they do come up here after us. But I don't want you to worry." He tried to make his voice reassuring. "We're safe here and we're smarter than they are. Don't you fret. We're going to get them and we're going to finish the job. After all, I have some people to avenge. And I'm a man who always finishes what he starts. Now don't you forget that."

He was speaking lightly to allay her

fears, and she was aware of that. She was also aware of his underlying self-confidence. It was hard to be afraid of anything when you were with someone like Dan Drage.

"I have something to avenge now, too," she said somberly. "I feel the need to get even for their killing Elmer."

Dan came to the back of the cave then and sat down on the gray dust floor beside Marie. He handed her her rifle and then he pulled out his Colt .44 and lay it in his lap, the barrel pointing toward the mouth of the cave.

XXI

"Why did you stay on here at the ranch and try to run it all by yourself?" Drage asked Marie softly as they sat in the dark cave together and waited.

"Oh, I don't really know," she said. "I guess it was easier than going someplace else and starting over. Everybody has to be someplace, you know." And she laughed softly at her own humor.

"So you have run this ranch all by yourself since your folks died?" he went on. "I certainly admire your courage."

"Well, I hire extra help during round-up time," she said. "I couldn't do that alone. And then I've had Elmer as my permanent helper. Kind of a foreman without any hands to supervise."

Drage felt her shudder against him for a moment at the mention of the old-timer.

"Poor Elmer," she went on, her voice trembling. "He never hurt anybody in his whole life. He was only trying to protect me when he went after the man with the butcher knife."

"Unfortunately," Drage said, "it isn't always the good man who wins out in the end, although it would be nice if things worked out that way."

"Well," Marie said, "that's true. I just don't know what I'm going to do without Elmer. I've relied on him so much. I don't know how I'm going to run the ranch by myself."

Suddenly, Dan gripped her arm and she knew that he was telling her to be silent. Some of the leaves and brush at the mouth of the cave were rustling. It was not a loud noise, but it was a definite rustling sound all the same.

As quietly as a ghost, Dan Drage left Marie Sandoval's side.

He moved along the wall of the cave, stepping softly and quickly to the mouth. No one was directly in front of the cave, so Drage slipped silently outside and into the dark night.

A few moments earlier, Tubby Gideon had been standing on the hill off to one side of the cave. He had then started to head inside, pistol in hand, stepping on the leaves and branches. As he did so, he knew that the sounds would alert the people inside of the cave, so he immediately backed off and waited on the hillside indecisively.

Walt was further down the hill and Tubby hated to make a definite move on his own. He needed to have his brother telling him what to do, how to do it, and where to go next. So he merely stood there and did nothing.

Dan Drage crouched low on the hillside almost directly in front of Tubby, but, because he was low and it was dark, Tubby did not see him. Drage tensed his leg muscles and then, like a steel spring uncoiling, he sprang toward Tubby Gideon.

Tubby did not know what hit him. Before he realized it, he was not only on the ground but unconscious as well.

Drage looked around quickly at the moonlit landscape. He did not know where Walt Gideon was, but he had surveyed the area right near the cave and he was fairly sure that Walt was not very close by.

Quickly, silently, Drage slipped back to the rear of the cavern. Marie Sandoval gasped as he suddenly clutched her hand.

"It's me," he reassured her softly. "Come quickly."

She got to her feet in an instant. Then she allowed herself to be led out of the cave. She made every effort to be as silent as he was, but she did not quite succeed.

At one point she accidentally dislodged a small rock and it clattered down the hillside.

Walt Gideon had heard, in the clear night air, the sound of Drage's encounter with Tubby near the mouth of the cave.

A little later Walt heard the small dislodged rock as it rolled down the hillside.

Walt swung his six-gun toward the sound of the rock. He was about to fire his gun, but he was not sure what he was hearing. The sound might be Tubby crossing the hillside. Even though he had told Tubby to stay by the cave, he could never be sure what his scatterbrained brother would do.

And Walt knew that if he fired aimlessly, he would give away his position to their adversary.

So Walt merely stood and waited, and the dark night became mostly silent again, with only the sound of the night birds breaking the stillness.

Walt Gideon stood and waited a while longer.

Finally, he could bear the suspense no longer. He had sent Tubby up to smoke the two people out of the cave and obviously Tubby had failed.

Yes, Tubby had failed as usual, Walt thought bitterly.

It didn't seem to him that Tubby could ever do anything right. If Walt wanted something done, he had to do it himself, or so it seemed to him. And now things were further complicated by the fact that Walt didn't know exactly what had happened to his brother.

Walt decided he had to make some kind of move. He could not just wait in the dark forever.

So he began to head slowly up the hillside toward the cave, trying to move as quietly as possible. When he got near the cave, he heard a moan. He kept his pistol ready, pointing it in the direction of the moaning sound. And he himself moved slowly in that same direction.

Then Walt saw the figure of a man lying on the ground in the darkness. Walt was wary, not knowing who it was, not knowing if it were a trick. He aimed his gun at the man on the ground and advanced cautiously. At last he bent over the man and then was able to identify him.

"Tubby! Tubby! What happened?"

Walt reached down and shook his brother. He slapped his face lightly, trying to bring him around. Slowly Tubby Gideon opened his eyes and looked at Walt.

He regained his senses and slowly he sat up with the help of his brother.

Tubby shook his head and then he fingered his jaw bone. Drage had given him a hard punch to the jaw. It hurt like fury. It didn't feel to him as if it were broken, but it was surely swollen.

"What happened?" Walt repeated.

"I don't know," Tubby mumbled. "I was just standing in front of that cave and all of a sudden something hit me. I don't know what happened."

Walt Gideon sat down on the ground beside his brother and began to curse quietly but fluently.

"That means that they got out of the cave," Walt said. "That means that they've gotten away from here. I was hoping that we could trap them in that cave."

"So what are we going to do now?" Tubby asked as he continued rubbing his tender jaw.

"We're not going to do a cockeyed thing for the rest of the night," Walt told him. "We're just going to sit here and one of us is going to stay awake all of the time so that they don't sneak up on us and pop you in the jaw again."

Tubby grumbled, but he didn't say anything in response. He didn't like the idea of sitting on the barren hillside in the cold of the night. And, besides, his jaw hurt.

But Walt was the boss, so Tubby found a large rock to brace his back against and sat down to wait out the night.

XXII

Dan Drage guided Marie Sandoval down the hill in the moonlit night and he took her to the far side of the barn. The corral with all the horses was there, and Drage spread some hay close to the side of the barn and suggested to Marie that they get some sleep.

"I'd rather be in the house in my bed," she said. "I don't know if I can sleep here

153

and now. Can you?"

He smiled at her.

"I've learned to catch a few winks when I can. If we sleep out here close to the horses, they'll alert us if anyone comes by. They'll make a noise and we'll know if someone is snooping around here. It's almost as good as being surrounded by dry brush and leaves."

He looked down at the hay. "I think that it will be warm enough here by the side of the barn," he said, his manner very casual.

Marie looked at him in wonderment. "How can you sleep with those two men out there, waiting to murder us?" she asked.

He looked at her and smiled, and she could see his smile even in the dark.

"My dear," he said, "we need our rest. That's why we're going to sleep here by the horses. With them around, we can sleep soundly. Now you don't have to sleep if you don't want to. You can keep watch while I sleep."

And he said that with a grin that

couldn't help but irritate her. Yet she said nothing.

He fluffed up the hay and lay down on it. With a sigh of weariness and resignation, she too lay down on the hay. But she could not relax. Marie was extremely worried about the two Gideon brothers. She was sure that they would try to sneak up on them in the night. It seemed impossible for her to close her eyes.

She cradled the Winchester .76 in her arms as she lay there and nervously watched the horses moving around behind the fence of the corral.

Soon she became aware that Dan Drage was beginning to breathe very deeply and she realized that he had fallen sound asleep.

How can he do that! Marie thought in exasperation. Here we are at the mercy of two killers, and he just lies down and goes to sleep without a care in the world!

Marie Sandoval dozed off herself after several listless hours. But she did not sleep very deeply or very long. Dan was still asleep when she woke up.

Finally, though, as the rosy light of dawn began to appear above the rolling hills, Dan Drage suddenly opened his eyes and was wide awake.

"Were you able to get some sleep?" he asked her softly in his deep tone.

"No, I didn't get much," she said, the resentment thinly veiled in her voice. "But you obviously did."

He smiled. "I saw no reason not to," he said. "I felt that I might as well."

"Well, I'm sure you might as well. I'm glad one of us slept well," she responded rather huffily.

He smiled at her again. But she was not about to be influenced by his pleasant smile. At least not under the circumstances surrounding them. He sat up, stretched, and looked around him, then checked both their guns to make sure they were in working order.

He smiled at her again and received no answering smile in return.

"All right," Dan said, his tone becoming serious and businesslike, "they're going to come back for their horses. That's something they have to do. The thing for us to do is to prepare a welcome for them."

"All right," Marie agreed. "What do you want me to do?"

As Dan Drage was telling Marie Sandoval what his plan was for the day, Walt and Tubby Gideon were making their way slowly down the rock-strewn hillside, heading toward the house.

"Jeez," Tubby complained, "I darned near froze to death up on that hill last night."

"Oh, quit your griping," Walt said. "You're all right. It wasn't that bad."

"Well, I think it was," Tubby said defensively. Then he abruptly changed the subject. "Walt, what do you think happened to Frank?"

Walt shrugged. "Who knows?" he snapped impatiently. "They may have caught him in the town. We'll go down and get our horses and then we'll ride back by the town. Maybe we can break him out of jail."

"We can't go back into that town!" Tubby said nervously, wiping his forehead with his sleeve. "Those people will be looking for us. They'll throw us in jail too."

"Oh, we'll just keep out of sight," Walt assured him. "Don't you worry about it. Let me worry for both of us. But the first thing we've got to do is go down there and get our horses out of that corral."

"Do you think it's safe?" the ever-nervous Tubby asked. "Where do you think the man and the woman are?"

"They're probably in the house. Probably still asleep," Walt said. "That's why we came down the hill so early, to catch them before they got up. But just to be sure," he went on, "why don't I circle around the barn toward the corral first to see if we can surprise them—if they happen to be out and around? After you've given me a few minutes to get set up, then you come around the other side. That way, in case they happen to be outside, we'll catch them on both sides. They won't be expecting that."

"Well, I don't know," Tubby responded, wiping his face with his dirty sleeve. "I don't think we ought to get into any gunplay around here if we can avoid it."

"We won't if we can avoid it," Walt said with finely pointed sarcasm in his voice. "But we're not going to walk out of here without horses either. Now do as you're told for once!"

XXIII

After his exchange with Tubby, Walt
Gideon drew his six-gun and slowly and
carefully made his way across the flat
ground toward the whitewashed barn.
Other than the milling horses, there was
no sound nor sign of life in the ranch yard.

Walt made sure as he walked that he
did not turn his back toward the house,
since he was still assuming that the man
and the woman had spent their night in

the house and were still there.

As he rounded the corner of the barn, he looked quickly around him, but he could see no one. The horses were grazing quietly behind the rails of the wooden fence. As far as Walt Gideon could tell, there was no one else around and nothing appeared to be out of place or out of the ordinary. The saddles were slung over the top rail of the fence just as Tubby had left them when he had unsaddled the horses the day before.

Walt looked at the horses for a few minutes. Then he turned away, and the back door of the white barn opened quietly. The tall, gaunt frame of Dan Drage was standing just behind the dark opening.

"Hold it right there, Gideon," Drage said in his deep, penetrating voice.

Although Drage already had his six-gun drawn, he did not anticipate that Walt Gideon would react as rapidly as he did. Gideon turned and quickly snapped a shot off from his own six-gun. The bullet struck the side of the barn just inches from Drage's head, showering him with splinters.

Drage returned the fire immediately
and the bullet from his Colt .44 whined
over the head of Walt Gideon as Gideon
dived over the top rail of the fence surrounding the corral, hitting the ground,
and rolling away in the dirt.

Drage stepped out of the barn to get a
clearer shot at the other man. Just as he
stepped from the protection of the building, Tubby Gideon came around the other
end of the barn. Drage did not see him
because he was looking for Walt.

Tubby leveled his revolver, but his
nerves were getting the better of him. He
reached up to steady the gun with his left
hand. Then there was the instant roar of
a weapon.

But it was not Tubby Gideon's revolver
that had fired. It was the Winchester .76
in the hands of Marie Sandoval that had
blasted out its message of death. Marie
was standing off to one side of the barn,
behind a cottonwood tree, where neither
of the Gideon brothers had seen her.

Tubby Gideon staggered as the rifle slug
struck him. He tried to recover and bring
his six-gun back to bear on Dan Drage.

Only, Drage had turned after Marie had fired and, as Tubby tried to aim his revolver, Drage squeezed the trigger on his own pistol.

The heavy gun roared and the hapless Tubby Gideon collapsed on the dusty ground. His body quivered briefly as he lay there. Then he was still.

Drage turned quickly and waved his gun toward the corral, trying to spot Walt Gideon again.

"I saw him run out the other side of the corral, Dan," Marie Sandoval said. "It looked to me like he was headed in the direction of the house."

Drage holstered his still-smoking six-gun and walked over to Marie. The Winchester in her right hand was pointed toward the ground now. The act of shooting had apparently left her feeling somewhat drained. Her face was slightly pale as she looked up into Dan's dark eyes.

"Thanks for the backup, ma'am," he said with a slight bow. "You undoubtedly saved my life."

She looked down at the body of Tubby Gideon, and she shuddered.

"You're welcome," she said. "I—I've never done anything like this in my life. I've never shot a man before."

Drage patted her on the shoulder, trying to be of comfort to her, trying to help her through a rough time.

"Everyone has doubts and guilt when they shoot someone," he told her. "It's always worse when you shoot the first person. But most of us—most normal people—get bothered whenever we shoot someone. I do it, but it always bothers me." Then he smiled at her. "If it's any consolation to you," he said, "I think you picked the right time to shoot someone for the first time."

She smiled wanly at him. "I'm glad I did you some good," she said. "What do we do now?"

"I think we should get around to where we can watch the house from the corner of the barn," Drage told her. "I'm sure that Walt'll head for the house to pick up the saddlebags that have the money from the bank in them."

"Oh, that's right," she said. "That's why he needed to get back into the house. But what will we do then?"

Dan smiled down at her again and she was sure that she could see a hint of impishness in his face, a look of mischief that made him seem like a boy.

"Well, he'll go into the house after the saddlebags, but he won't stay in the house for long after he gets there," Drage told her.

"Why is that?" she asked. "Because he'll come out with the saddlebags?"

"No, that's not quite what I meant. He'll come out quickly," Dan said, the mischievous smile still on his face, "because the saddlebags are no longer inside of the house."

XXIV

Marie looked at Dan incredulously. This man was really a wonder. She found it easy to believe the stories that had sprung up about him.

"How did you manage to get the bags out of the house?" she asked. "When in the world did you carry them out? I've been with you all of the time."

"I carried them out of the house with me after I had untied you and just as we were leaving for the cave," he told her.

"But I was with you all of that time," she protested. "I didn't see you doing that."

"You had other things on your mind," he said. "You weren't watching my every move."

"But where on earth did you put them?" she persisted. "You didn't carry them up to the cave with us."

"Oh, no," he assured her. "They're really not that far from the house. I chucked them underneath the front porch just as we left the house. But, of course, Walt Gideon won't know about that any more than you did."

They rounded the corner of the barn where the house was in full view and then they stopped and watched the place closely. Dan Drage did not believe that Gideon would stay inside for any length of time, especially after the man had discovered that the saddlebags were not in the front room where he had left them.

Soon enough Walt left the house by the back door—and he spotted the pair.

"Hey, out there by the barn," the remaining Gideon brother called out. "I don't want any more trouble with you. I don't want no more gunplay. I just want my saddlebags and my horse. Give them to me and I'll be riding on. I'll leave you alone and you leave me alone."

Ordinarily, thought Drage, that would have been a pretty fair exchange. Under the present circumstances, though, he could not accept it.

"I'll just bet he'd like his saddlebags and his horse," Drage said to Marie. "That would be just fine with him."

"Maybe we ought to give him the saddlebags and let him ride on his way," Marie said. "That way we'd be rid of him forever."

"You know," he said solemnly, "there are two reasons why that isn't the best idea you ever had. The first one is that man is a killer. I've sworn to avenge my brother's death and I mean to do so."

"Do you have to kill him?" she asked.

"Not necessarily," Dan responded. "I would be willing to take him in to the marshal at Colorado Springs and stay around here to see him hanged. But I'm not at all sure that Walt Gideon is the type of man who will stand still for being taken in."

"No," she answered reflectively, "I suppose not."

"The second reason I don't think we should give him his saddlebags and let him ride away," Drage went on, "is that's not his money. It belongs to the bank."

"Oh, I know. I know," Marie said. "I'm sorry I even suggested such a thing. I know we can't let him get away. It's just that— well, it's just that I'm so nervous, and he's so dangerous. The fact that I've killed a man and the fact that we have this killer trapped in the house. It's just so—so unnerving. What if he kills you?"

Dan put his arm around her shoulders.

"I'm sorry," he said. "I know that you're not used to all this. Just trust me. Please?"

"Hey, out there," Gideon called. "Do you hear me? Let's live and let live. Just let me ride on and I'll never come this way again."

Drage stuck his head just far enough around the corner of the barn so that he could be sure the man would hear him.

"No deal!" he yelled back. "The money

in those saddlebags isn't yours. It belongs
to the bank."

"Are you a lawman?" Gideon asked.

"No," Drage yelled back. "That's not my
interest in this. Aside from the money, I
can't let you get away. You have to answer to me for some things."

"How can I answer to you?" Gideon
yelled at him. "I don't even *know* you.
What is your interest in me? What's your
name?"

"My name is Dan Drage!"

Walt Gideon was still puzzled. "Sure,
I've heard of you," he said, "but what do
I have to do with you? We've never met."

"No," Drage acknowledged, "we've
never met. But the man and woman you
killed outside the bank at Cheyenne were
my brother and his wife."

Walt Gideon now was silent. He under-
stood.

Well, if Dan Drage wouldn't make a
deal, he would have to kill him and the
woman too. There was no other way. And
Walt knew he was the man who could do
it. He surely was.

XXV

Drage gestured with his hand, indicating that Marie should stay behind the barn.

"Watch out," he told her softly. "There's going to be gunplay here and I don't want you to get hurt."

She pressed his arm lightly.

"I—I'm concerned about you too, Dan," she told him. "I want to help you any way I can."

"Okay. I'll let you help me," he agreed. "But right now I want you to stay back. I don't want you to get hit. All right?"

"All right."

At that point a six-gun roared from the house. Drage saw the flash of the gunfire and the smoke from the revolver at the back door. The slug chipped the corner of the whitewashed barn and screamed away in a ricochet that tore through the desert air.

Drage eased his head around the barn corner until he could see the house. His Colt .44 answered the challenge with its own deep-throated roar, and Drage could see the gray dust fly from the doorjamb as the bullet from his gun hit the edge of the door very close to Walt Gideon. He had not hit Gideon, though.

Gideon went in and slammed the back door of the house after Drage's bullet came close. Drage stood at the corner of the barn, frozen in his position, his six-gun pointed toward the house.

"I think he must be headed for the front door of the house," Drage told Marie over his shoulder. "You stay here and keep your rifle trained on the back door. If he comes out this way, you shoot him."

"But—" she began.

"No!" he said with firmness in his voice. "There is no argument. If he comes out of the back door, you shoot him. Promise me, Marie!"

"All right, Dan," she said meekly. "I promise."

"I'm going around to the front door," he said. "If he comes out that way, like I think he will, then I'll take him there, and you won't have anything to worry about."

Dan ran toward the stone wall at the corner of the house. All was quiet. Then, as Dan moved still closer to the house, he saw that Walt Gideon had just stepped out the front door onto the small porch.

Gideon fired his pistol and Dan Drage felt a sharp pain searing his left upper arm.

Drage dove for the ground, his long, lean body hitting the front lawn and rolling over. As he came up from his shoulder roll, he still had his Colt .44 in his hand.

While Walt was aiming again, Drage shot him neatly in the chest. Gideon's shirt front suddenly blossomed a bright crimson. He staggered back with the shock, dropped the six-gun from his rapidly numbing fingers, and fell off the porch onto the grass.

Drage noted that Gideon's body had crumpled only a few feet from the saddlebags under the porch, the saddlebags which contained the money Gideon had stolen from the Wells Fargo Bank in Helaman, Colorado.

Drage struggled to his feet. He slowly holstered his still-smoking weapon and walked slowly to where the body of Walt Gideon lay. He looked at the man he had been pursuing for a few solemn moments. No, he did not feel good about the shooting. But justice had been done.

Drage bent down and pulled the saddlebags from underneath the porch.

"Dan! Dan! Are you all right?" Marie Sandoval called from the back of the house.

"Around here," he yelled back to her. "Yes. I'm all right."

He merely stood there and eagerly waited until she ran breathlessly around

the house. She threw herself into his arms
and embraced him. He put his right arm
around her, since he had the saddlebags
in his left hand. He squeezed her gently,
warmly.

Then she moved back a step, her face
slightly flushed.

"I'm sorry," she said. "You must think
me awfully forward. It's just that I'm so
happy to see you're all right."

"It's all right," he replied with a smile.
"I'm not often greeted that enthusiastically. It's real nice."

She blushed again and then she saw the
blood on his left arm.

"You're hurt!" she exclaimed.

"It's really nothing," he assured her. "He
creased me with a slug. It's only a flesh
wound."

"I'm so glad it isn't serious," she said.
Then she paused a moment. "What are
you going to do now?"

"Well, I'll bury your hired man, Elmer.
I think we should do that first. Then I'll
take the bodies of the two Gideon brothers
into town and return the money to the
bank."

He looked at her as though he had something else on his mind. Then he went on:

"After I deliver these packages to the town of Helaman, I guess I'll be riding on."

"Do you have to?" she asked plaintively.

He looked at her questioningly. She put her hand gently on his arm and looked up into his face.

"I don't have anyone to help me here on the ranch now," she said. "I'd consider it a real favor if you'd stay here and help me run this place."

He smiled at her beautiful brave face.

"I'm not sure you'd really want me," he said. "I'm still a target for every other gunslinger who tries his luck. I just don't know if I'm in any position to settle down."

"I'm willing to chance it if you are," Marie said, returning his smile. "Why don't we just try it for a couple of months? If it doesn't work, you can move on."

He took her hand in his.

"Lady," he said, "you've got yourself a deal. I'll go and take care of things I have to do, and then I'll be right back. And if you don't like my work in a couple of months, you can fire me."

"All right," she agreed. "As long as we can work together, we'll be a team."

He squeezed her hand. Then he turned and started to do the things he needed to do. Meanwhile, something told him their team just might—with some luck—last a real long time.